QUILTING ROW BY ROW

27 Skill-Building Techniques

Jeanette White & Erin Hamilton

T0308541

C&T PUBLISHING

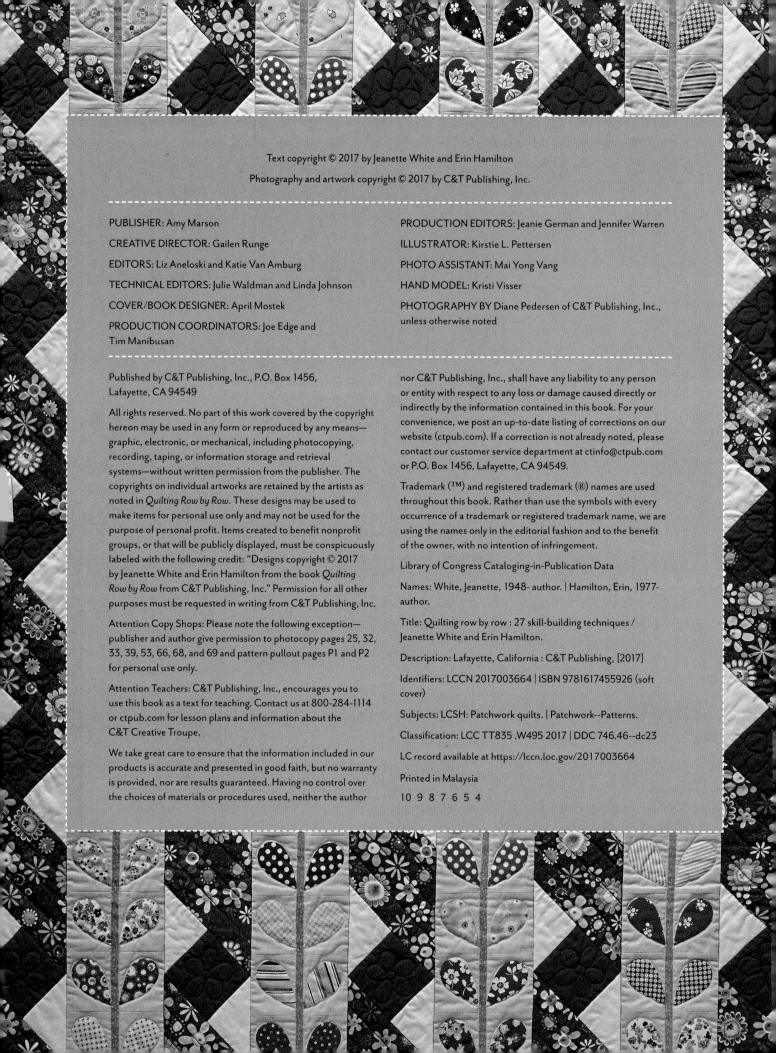

Text copyright © 2017 by Jeanette White and Erin Hamilton

Photography and artwork copyright © 2017 by C&T Publishing, Inc.

PUBLISHER: Amy Marson

CREATIVE DIRECTOR: Gailen Runge

EDITORS: Liz Aneloski and Katie Van Amburg

TECHNICAL EDITORS: Julie Waldman and Linda Johnson

COVER/BOOK DESIGNER: April Mostek

PRODUCTION COORDINATORS: Joe Edge and
Tim Manibusan

PRODUCTION EDITORS: Jeanie German and Jennifer Warren

ILLUSTRATOR: Kirstie L. Pettersen

PHOTO ASSISTANT: Mai Yong Vang

HAND MODEL: Kristi Visser

PHOTOGRAPHY BY Diane Pedersen of C&T Publishing, Inc.,
unless otherwise noted

Published by C&T Publishing, Inc., P.O. Box 1456,
Lafayette, CA 94549

All rights reserved. No part of this work covered by the copyright hereon may be used in any form or reproduced by any means—graphic, electronic, or mechanical, including photocopying, recording, taping, or information storage and retrieval systems—without written permission from the publisher. The copyrights on individual artworks are retained by the artists as noted in *Quilting Row by Row*. These designs may be used to make items for personal use only and may not be used for the purpose of personal profit. Items created to benefit nonprofit groups, or that will be publicly displayed, must be conspicuously labeled with the following credit: "Designs copyright © 2017 by Jeanette White and Erin Hamilton from the book *Quilting Row by Row* from C&T Publishing, Inc." Permission for all other purposes must be requested in writing from C&T Publishing, Inc.

Attention Copy Shops: Please note the following exception—publisher and author give permission to photocopy pages 25, 32, 33, 39, 53, 66, 68, and 69 and pattern pullout pages P1 and P2 for personal use only.

Attention Teachers: C&T Publishing, Inc., encourages you to use this book as a text for teaching. Contact us at 800-284-1114 or ctpub.com for lesson plans and information about the C&T Creative Troupe.

We take great care to ensure that the information included in our products is accurate and presented in good faith, but no warranty is provided, nor are results guaranteed. Having no control over the choices of materials or procedures used, neither the author nor C&T Publishing, Inc., shall have any liability to any person or entity with respect to any loss or damage caused directly or indirectly by the information contained in this book. For your convenience, we post an up-to-date listing of corrections on our website (ctpub.com). If a correction is not already noted, please contact our customer service department at ctinfo@ctpub.com or P.O. Box 1456, Lafayette, CA 94549.

Trademark (™) and registered trademark (®) names are used throughout this book. Rather than use the symbols with every occurrence of a trademark or registered trademark name, we are using the names only in the editorial fashion and to the benefit of the owner, with no intention of infringement.

Library of Congress Cataloging-in-Publication Data

Names: White, Jeanette, 1948- author. | Hamilton, Erin, 1977-author.

Title: Quilting row by row : 27 skill-building techniques / Jeanette White and Erin Hamilton.

Description: Lafayette, California : C&T Publishing, [2017]

Identifiers: LCCN 2017003664 | ISBN 9781617455926 (soft cover)

Subjects: LCSH: Patchwork quilts. | Patchwork--Patterns.

Classification: LCC TT835 .W495 2017 | DDC 746.46--dc23

LC record available at https://lccn.loc.gov/2017003664

Printed in Malaysia

10 9 8 7 6 5 4

Contents

Introduction

A few years ago, we made a beautiful row quilt with a group of students as a class. The group worked on one row a month, with the goal to finish the quilt by the end of the year. Many of our students were complete beginners when we started. We had such a great time and could not believe how much everyone learned by the end of the year. We decided that not only was our row quilt beautiful when completed but that it was a fantastic teaching quilt.

So here we are now, using it in this book to teach you many of our favorite quilting techniques and tips that really work. Each row chapter has instructions to complete one row, but you can make multiples of a single row and create an entire quilt.

Our hope is that you continue to make quilt after quilt of your own designs using the individual row patterns in different ways. The possibilities are endless!

Jeanette White and Erin Hamilton, also known as The Piper's Girls, with the current namesake of the business, Piper Dunlop

Getting Started

Getting Started with *Piper's Girls' Row Quilt*

You do not need to have a great deal of previous quilting experience to make our row quilt. The quilt is designed as a teaching tool to move your level of expertise from beginner to expert. (If you already fancy yourself an expert, we still think you will learn a lot.)

Each row uses different quilting techniques. The instructions for the rows are listed in order of difficulty level, so you will start with a simple row. By the end of the eleventh row, you will have learned valuable basic quilting techniques, as well as some specialized ones.

Note: The numbering of the rows pertains to the level of difficulty. The rows do not appear in the quilt in this numbered order.

This chapter covers some general skills and basic information you will use in all of the rows, as well as material requirements and preliminary cutting instructions.

Materials

FABRICS

Note: Below is a list of all the fabrics you will need to make the entire quilt.

Background, sashings, and inner borders: 4 yards of off-white solid (This amount allows for a little extra in case of mistakes. We all make those, right?) Cut the long length-of-grain pieces first; then cut the smaller pieces. See Cutting Borders, Sashing, and Long Rows (page 13).

For use throughout the quilt: 36 fat quarters in a variety of colors and print sizes (6 should be green in a range of hues. Scraps of these will be used for the Row 11 appliqués.)

Row 2: ¼ yard of red print

Rows 2 and 3: ¼ yard of red solid

Row 7: ¼ yard of pink print

¼ yard of orange polka dot

¼ yard of teal solid

Row 8: ⅓ yard of red print

⅓ yard of light blue print

¼ yard of yellow solid

¼ yard of pink print

Row 11: 1½ yards of green micro print for grass (You will have a lot left over. We suggest this much to be able to cut on length of grain, page 10, and to avoid having an unsightly seam running through the center.)

Outer border: 2¼ yards of blue print (You will have extra, but you will need this amount to cut the borders on the length of grain, page 13.)

Backing: 4⅞ yards (Pick a fabric you love!)

TIP : A small clear 1˝ × 6˝ ruler is especially helpful for cutting the spokes.

Binding: 1⅛ yards (We used a small black gingham check.)

Batting: 65˝ × 86˝ (We love the bamboo batting!)

Medium rickrack: 8 yards in red to add into the binding (*optional*)

Finished quilt: 58˝ × 79˝

Row 9

Row 2

Row 3

Row 6

Row 1

Row 11

Row 8

Row 5

Row 7

Row 4

Row 10

Piper's Girls' Row Quilt

Row 9

Row 2

Row 3

Row 6

Row 1

Row 11

Row 8

Row 5

Row 7

Row 4

Row 10

TOOLS AND NOTIONS

We list our favorite brands in parenthesis following each item.

Rotary cutter (OLFA): 45 mm or 60 mm

Cutting mat (OLFA): 18˝ × 24˝

Rotary cutting rulers (Omnigrid): 6½˝ × 24˝ and 4˝ × 8˝

Clear ruler: 1˝ × 6˝

Self-adhesive sandpaper tabs: Stick them to the wrong side of the rulers in a 3˝ grid to prevent sliding when cuts are made. They are a super cheap addition that you won't ever want to go without once you have tried them.

Small scissors (Omnigrid 4˝ needlecraft)

Off-white thread (Aurifil): 100% cotton thread for piecing

Clear monofilament thread (Superior)

Extra-fine glass-head pins (Clover)

Pincushion: especially one that looks as great as it functions

¼˝ presser foot: If you do not already have one, check to see if one is available for your machine. Look for one that is as flat as possible and easy to see around. Never use the lines on your throat plate or masking tape; they are not very accurate.

Sewing machine #80 needle (Schmetz): This will work best for most of your stitching. Unless otherwise noted, this is your default needle.

Sewing machine #60 or #65 needle (Schmetz): This will work best for the appliqué rows.

Sewing machine #90 needle: This will work best for Rows 4–6.

Darning needle and a light color quilting thread: for Row 9

Chenille #20 needle and embroidery floss: red for Rows 3 and 11; 3 shades of green and 2 shades each of blue, tan, dark gray, and yellow for Row 11

Tapered awl or stiletto (Clover): One of the many uses for this tool is to guide the fabrics precisely under the presser foot while stitching.

Laundry sizing spray (Magic Sizing—Light Body): Available in the laundry section of the grocery store, this is a must. It gives the fabric extra body, making it much easier to work with.

Mechanical pencil

Extra-Fine Permanent Marker (Sharpie)

Fabric glue stick (Apliquick)

Appliqué basting glue (Roxanne Glue-Baste-It)

Cotton swabs

Medium-weight vellum paper: 24 sheets for Rows 3, 5, and 6

Tiny black beads: 12 for bird's eyes in Row 5

Template plastic: 3 sheets for Rows 5 and 6

Medium-weight interfacing (Apliquick): about 1½ yards for Row 11

Tweezers and awl: for Row 11 (We like the Apliquick Rod tool.)

Freezer paper: for Row 11 (reverse appliqué)

Great tools make all the difference!

Fabric Grainline

In this book, we reference grainline a lot. It is important to understand the properties of the fabrics that you are working with. There are three grainlines on fabric: width (WOF = width of fabric, which runs across from selvage to selvage), length (LOG = length of grain, which runs along the selvage), and bias (diagonal).

To quickly see the difference in how these three grains behave, try to stretch and pull a piece of fabric on the width, length, and bias. You can instantly see how much stronger and less stretchy the LOG is than the WOF. You will also notice how stretchy the bias is.

Although many patterns say to cut borders and sashings on the WOF, we disagree. A financial savings on fabric is usually the reason for this, but it is penny-wise and pound-foolish. The WOF (cross grain) stretches and is only about 40˝–42˝ wide once the selvage is cut off. This means you will have a lot of distortions due to stretch and seams showing in the sashings and borders. If the sashings and

borders are on the LOG, the quilt will square up effort-lessly because that grainline doesn't stretch when it is stitched and pressed. For this reason, we suggest that you cut the long pieces of the off-white background fabric first to ensure you have enough fabric to cut them on the LOG (page 13).

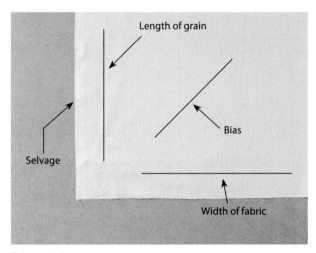

Fabric grainlines

Prewashing Fabrics

If you buy your fabric at an independent store that sells high-quality fabrics, prewashing is not necessary. It changes the texture and makes fabric more difficult to work with. If you are worried about colors running, just spritz the fabric with a little pure white vinegar, and iron dry.

Pressing Effectively

We suggest using your iron's wool setting. Because you will be pressing the same areas several times over the course of creating the blocks and rows, the fabric will become over-pressed if you use a cotton setting. Steam is also very helpful.

You may have heard this a million times before, but make sure to press rather than iron. Always use up-and-down motions and keep the movement of the iron to a minimum when it is in contact with the fabric. Pressing is done to set the fabric—as opposed to ironing, which is using heat, steam, and motion to smooth out wrinkles.

Pressing Seam Allowances

Seam allowances are pressed together to one side, not open, unless otherwise noted. This is done to give the seams strength and makes it unnecessary to match thread color. The way you press seams can play an important role in a quilt's finished look.

1. Lay the seam horizontally, right side up in front of you. Place the sole of the iron about 1˝ in front of the seam, apply a little pressure, and move forward over the seam.

2. When you feel the iron go over a little bump (the seam), hold the iron in place for 10 seconds. Remember to press, not iron.

Place the iron sole 1˝ in front of the seam, apply pressure, and move forward over the seam.

Seam allowance pressed to one side

Seam Allowances

Seam allowances are ¼˝, unless otherwise noted.

Make sure you line up the raw edges of the fabric with the outer edge of the ¼˝ foot when stitching.

> **TIP** For accuracy, always use a ¼˝ foot on your machine as a guide rather than the throat plate or a piece of tape.

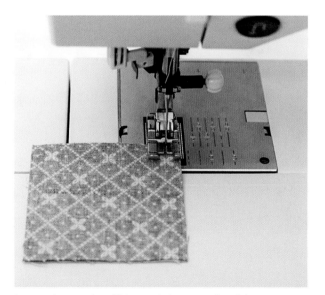

Line up the raw edge of fabric with the outer edge of the presser foot.

Accurate Cutting

You will need a rotary cutter, a 6½″ × 24″ ruler, and a cutting mat. Before cutting, give the fabric a light press (see Pressing Effectively, page 10), and fold it in half selvage to selvage so the fold is on the LOG. Fold again if you want to cut through four layers.

When using a rotary cutter, it is very important that you always place your index finger on the gridded area on the handle. It stops your hand from wobbling and also reduces the stress on your wrist when cutting.

It is very important to hold a rotary cutter correctly.

Always maintain a little pressure with the blade against the edge of the ruler. Make cuts by pushing the blade away from you. Never use a back-and-forth sawing motion or pull the blade toward you. You can save time by cutting through multiple layers.

The first cut is called a "true cut." It is very important for this cut to be accurate because all of the cuts that follow are based off this cut. Use the ruler as a T-square. To obtain a square and accurate width-of-fabric cut, you will use the fold of the fabric.

Lay the ruler on the fabric with any line on the fold. Trim off enough to make sure you are going through both layers of fabric. Place your noncutting hand flat in the middle of the ruler, and make a cut, applying enough pressure to the rotary cutter to cleanly cut both layers of fabric at once. This is your true cut.

Make a true cut.

Determine the size of strip you want to cut. Measure twice, checking both ends and the middle of the ruler to make sure your desired cut measurement is consistent and accurate for the entire length of the ruler. Cut. The fabric should not be moved after the cutting process has begun; if the placement of the fabric needs to be moved to cut again, move the entire mat. After you have made several cuts, always make a new true cut.

The various shapes needed for block construction all start with cutting WOF strips first. The second cuts create the final shapes required.

Cutting Borders, Sashing, and Long Rows

OFF-WHITE SOLID

It is very important to cut the borders first and sashings second on the LOG. If you wait until you have started making the rows, you may cut into the length and will not have enough to cut the borders on the LOG.

BORDERS

1. Press the whole 4-yard piece of off-white fabric (see Accurate Cutting, previous page).

2. Cut a rectangle WOF × 80˝.

3. Cut off the selvage.

4. Fold it in half twice, crosswise. You should now have a folded piece WOF × 20˝ across. This is done so that you can make a single cut for accuracy as opposed to moving the ruler down the 80˝ length.

5. Cut 4 border strips 1½˝ × 80˝. Label and set aside.

SASHING AND ROWS

1. Cut the 80˝ length of fabric to WOF × 54˝. Fold in half twice, crosswise. You should now have a folded piece WOF × 13½˝ across.

2. Cut 1 strip 11½˝ × 54˝ LOG for the Row 11 background.

3. Cut 10 strips 1½˝ × 54˝ for the sashing. Label and set aside.

The remainder of the off-white fabric will be used in the rows whenever you are instructed to cut fabric for the background.

GREEN MICRO PRINT

Cut 1 strip 6˝ × 54˝ for the Row 11 grass.

Butting Seams, Pinning, and Stitching

Unless otherwise indicated, prepare and sew all seams in this fashion.

Butting Seams

1. Line up the raw edges of the fabric and the vertical seamline.

2. Intentionally misalign the vertical seamline by about ¼˝ by gripping the intersection of the vertical seamlines between your thumb and forefinger and sliding a little.

When you feel the intersection slide and lock into place, this means that the two vertical seamlines will line up perfectly with no interruptions and the seam allowances will be in opposing directions. This is called "butting the seams."

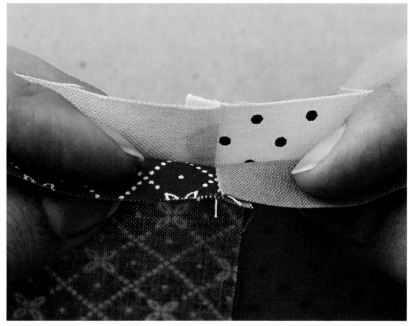

Butted seams

Pinning

1. Once the seams are correctly aligned, place a pin perpendicular to the raw edges. Make sure not to let go until you have pinned.

Pin perpendicular to the raw edges.

2. Pin through all layers of fabric, just to the left of the vertical seamline. Butting the seams this way will control the bulk issue without jeopardizing the strength of the seams or requiring matched thread.

3. Continue until you have pinned all the 4-way seam junctions.

Stitching

It is far more efficient to do all the pinning and then all the stitching as opposed to pinning and stitching individually.

Once you have pinned, begin stitching, making sure the raw edges are lining up with the right-hand edge of the presser foot. This is where an awl and extra-fine pins will be your best friends. Stitch over the pin holding the seam junction. When you have a seam allowance that is going away from you, hold it down with the point of an awl and guide it as it goes under the presser foot.

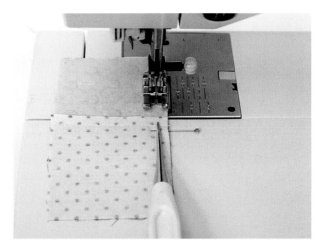

Use an awl to guide seams and keep them from flipping.

CHAIN PIECING

Stitch all the pieces one after another, without cutting the thread. After stitching the last piece, cut the threads that join the pieces to separate them.

Oops! Adjusting the Row Measurement

The most common "oops" with this quilt is an incorrect finished-width measurement. You will aim for 52½˝ on the first row. Because every row in this quilt is unique and some rows have quite a bit of piecing, it is virtually impossible to get the same exact finished size on each row. The height of the row won't really matter, but the width of each row needs to be the same for the quilt to fit together.

Note: For consistency, "width" refers to the side-to-side measurement of both the row and the quilt. "Length" is the top-to-bottom measurement of the quilt. "Height" is the short dimension of the row.

Don't panic! Find a large spot, preferably a hard surface like a floor or table. Lay the first row out once it's completed, and mark the width with a strip of masking tape at each end. These are not to be touched: from this point forward, this width will be what you will use to measure every subsequent row. This is far more accurate and a lot easier than measuring each row. We know this process is a bit different than the norm, but you will obtain better results for this project.

My Row Is Too Short

If the next row falls short in width according to your masking tape markers, determine the difference. Divide that number by 2, and add ¼˝ for your seam allowance. The result is your cutting measurement for the width of each "shim."

Make 2 side pieces or shims to stitch to the 2 ends.

For example, say you are 1¼˝ short on Row 2. Cut 2 rectangles, the row height × ⅞˝ (which is half of 1¼˝ plus ¼˝ for a seam allowance).

My Row Is Too Long

If the next row is too long, find the middle of the row and place a pin there. If the extra length is less than ¾˝, unpick and restitch the vertical seams, taking them in 1/16˝ at a time. If it is more than ¾˝, divide the number by 2 and cut the 2 ends of the row by that measurement.

Fabric Placement Mistakes

If you have made a mistake in color placement in a block, ask yourself, "Does it matter to me?" If it does, correct it. If it doesn't, move on and don't worry about it.

There are a few errors in our quilt (see if you can find them!), and we still love it! The main thing we want to emphasize is to have a good time while quilting. That's why we are doing this—to have fun!

Simple Embroidery Stitches

Simple embroidery can add a touch of detail.

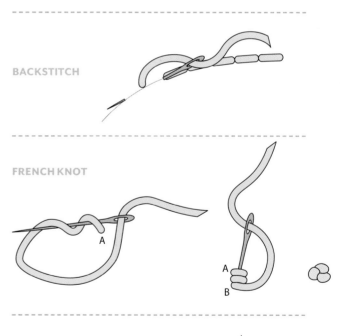

BACKSTITCH

FRENCH KNOT

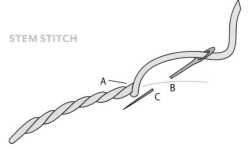

STEM STITCH

Row 1: Simple Patches

You will master the following techniques with this row:

- Accurate cutting (page 12)

- Exact ¼˝ seam allowance (page 11)

- Chain piecing (page 14)

- Controlling bulk by butting seams (page 13)

Materials

See Fabrics (page 6) for a complete list of suggested fabrics for this quilt.

Cutting

FAT QUARTERS

- Cut 1 rectangle 2½˝ × 5˝ from 26 fat quarters.

Stitching

Place 2 contrasting rectangles right sides together, and stitch using chain piecing to make 13 pairs.

Note: Contrast does not necessarily mean light and dark fabrics. For example, a red and a green with the same value still have great contrast.

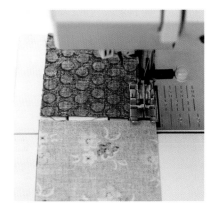

Chain piece rectangle sets into pairs.

Pressing

Press the seam allowances (page 11) on all 13 pairs in the same direction.

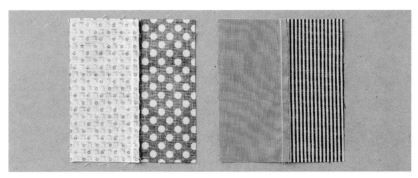

Press.

A Little More Cutting

Cut the 13 pairs into 2½˝ × 4½˝ units.

Cut the pairs into smaller units.

Layout

1. Lay out the units in 2 rows of 13.

> **TIP** What you want to accomplish is contrast between each pair and its neighbors. Avoid a concentration of colors. For example, you would not want to have reds all in one area.

2. Place a small piece of masking tape on each unit, and number them as shown.

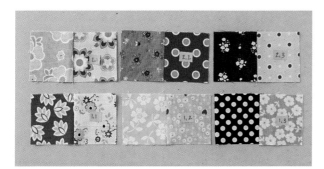

Lay out the units into two rows.

Stitching It All Together

Sewing the Rows

1. Stitch 2 units together, right sides facing, aligning the raw edges exactly. (There is no need to pin.)

2. Using the chain-piecing method, stitch together the double units until you have a row of 26.

3. Repeat Steps 1 and 2 (above) to stitch the second row of units.

4. Press the seam allowances of the first row to the right and the seam allowances of the second row to the left, so the seams will butt when you sew together the rows. You may be changing the direction of previously pressed seams in this step; that's okay.

Front

Back. Note the opposing direction of the pressed seams on each row.

Joining the Rows

1. Place the 2 rows right sides together. Pin, starting in the middle.

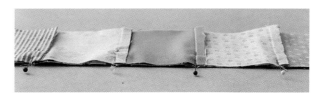

Perfectly butted seams

2. Stitch the entire pinned edge, joining together the 2 rows. With the right side facing up, press the last sewn seam allowance in one direction.

You have now completed Row 1 of your Row Quilt!

Row 2: Ribbons

You will master the following techniques with this row:

- Using the 45° angle on a ruler

- Stitching a diagonal seam

- Understanding the "dog-ear" and keeping points intact

Materials

See Fabrics (page 6) for a complete list of suggested fabrics for this quilt.

Cutting

RED PRINT

- Cut 1 strip 3⅜″ × WOF. Locate the 45° line on a ruler, and lay it on the long raw edge of the fabric near the end. Make a true cut at 45° across the width of the strip. Lay the ruler on the raw edge of the true cut.

- Cut 8 diamonds 3⅜″ wide.

Line up the ruler's 45° angle with the long raw edge of fabric.

Make a true cut at 45°.

Cut 8 diamonds 3⅜″ wide.

TIP | It is easier to cut all of these in a single layer; it will help to prevent any mistakes.

RED SOLID

- Cut 7 squares 2⅝″ × 2⅝″.

OFF-WHITE SOLID

- Cut 7 squares 2⅞″ × 2⅞″; then cut them in half diagonally, creating 14 triangles.

Cut squares in half diagonally.

Stitching It All Together

1. Pin an off-white triangle to one side of a red square at both corners. Note the triangle's orientation as shown in the photo. You will see that the triangle end is slightly longer than the side of the square at one end; this is called a "dog-ear." Match up the 90° corners, and begin stitching at this end.

2. Stitch. Press the seam allowance toward the red square. Make 7.

3. Repeat Steps 1 and 2 with a second upside down triangle on the opposite side of each square. Make 7.

Dog-ear

4. Place a red-and-cream unit on a red print diagonal strip, right sides together, aligning the corners as shown. Pin and stitch. Press the seam allowance toward the red print. Make 7.

Align the pieces as shown.

Stitch and press.

5. Pin the units into pairs, right sides together. Align the raw edges. Stitch.

6. Stitch the pairs together into a row. Stitch the remaining red print diagonal strip to the end of the row, so there is a red print diagonal strip at the start and finish of the row. Press.

> **TIP** One of the main objectives for this row is stitching perfect diagonal seams. The trick is keeping the dog-ear intact so you create a ¼˝ seam allowance for the next seam. This is the secret to keeping the points perfect. Aim for the points to hit right at the seamline.

7. Once you know the width the row should be (see Oops! Adjusting the Row Measurement, page 15), trim each end of the row at 90° using your masking tape markers for the correct width measurement. Make sure the ribbon units are centered in the row.

Row 3: Dresden

You will master the following techniques with this row:

- Creating points
- Machine appliqué
- Appliqué circles

Materials

See Fabrics (page 6) for a complete list of suggested fabrics for this quilt.

Templates

Make 2 or 3 vellum templates of each Dresden spoke pattern (page 25). If you use the same template for all 45 spokes, the edges tend to get a little worn, and it can affect your accuracy when cutting.

Cutting

FAT QUARTERS

- Using a mechanical pencil, trace Dresden spoke #1 twice on the wrong side of 23 fat quarters. (This will yield 46; 1 is extra.)

- Cut out 45 spokes exactly on the traced line.

  TIP : A small clear 1˝ × 6˝ ruler is especially helpful for cutting the spokes.

- Trace Dresden spoke #2 onto the wrong side of all 45 spokes, with spoke #2 lined up at the bottom edge of spoke #1. Make sure it is centered on the fabric so that the point is recessed ¼˝ down from the top line and there is an accurate ¼˝ seam allowance on both sides.

OFF-WHITE SOLID

- Cut 5 rectangles 10½˝ × 6˝.

Trace Dresden Spoke #2.

Making the Dresdens

1. Fold a spoke in half lengthwise, right sides together. Push a pin straight through both layers from top to bottom, aligning the 2 side points. Make sure these points match; then pin along the top edge.

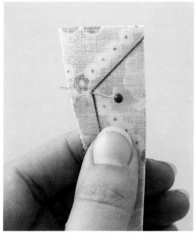

Fold a spoke in half, and push a pin through the points.

Back view of pin poking through at matching point

2. Machine stitch ¼˝ from the raw edge along the top.

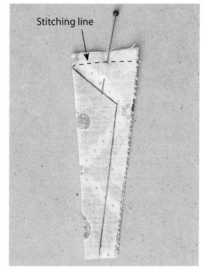

Stitching line

Machine stitch ¼˝ from the top raw edge.

3. Use a fabric glue stick to smear glue on the wrong side of the seam allowance, and finger-press it open. This will hold it in place.

Use a glue stick to press and hold the seam allowance open.

Note: If you simply press the seam allowance open rather than using the method in Step 3, it is very easy to press it the wrong way. It is difficult to remove the incorrect crease.

4. Turn the spoke right side out and press. Make 45.

TIP To get the points nice and sharp, use an awl to tease each point out from the right side. This is a far better way to get a perfect point than pushing it from the other side with something sharp—you are likely to poke a hole and damage the Dresden spoke that way.

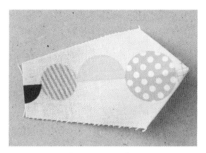

Turn the Dresden spoke right side out.

Putting the Spokes Together

1. Lay the spokes out in 5 blocks of 9 spokes.

2. Place the spokes right sides together, with the side points matching. Push a pin through the ¼˝ line on the top fabric to make sure the bottom fabric is lined up perfectly. Pin and stitch, backstitching at the outside edge.

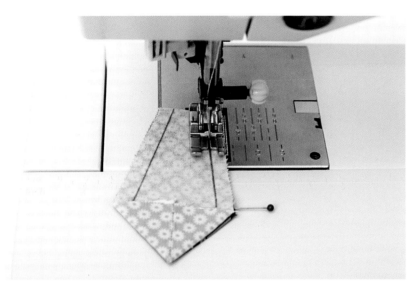

Spokes right sides together and lined up perfectly. Stitch.

3. Chainstitch the spokes of block 1 into pairs; then press all the seams open.

4. Stitch the pairs together, and stitch the remaining spoke to the end of the row. Make 5 Dresdens.

Back of stitched Dresden. Note that the seams are pressed open.

Note: To keep the fabric positions straight, you will need a system. Some quilters like to use their phones to photograph each block layout. We like to use masking tape to label each piece's position. For example, on block 1 it would read 1,1; 1,2; and so on. Block 2 would be 2,1; 2,2; and so on. In this way you can chainstitch, but the plates all have the balanced appearance that you chose in your layout.

Adding the Background

1. Fold 1 of the background rectangles in half widthwise (align the short sides), and lightly finger-press.

2. Place 1 Dresden on the background fabric so that the point of spoke 5 is aligned with the finger-pressed line and the raw edges of the first and last spokes are lined up with the bottom raw edge of the background fabric. Pin in place.

3. Use appliqué adhesive to place tiny, equally spaced dots along the seamlines and at the raw edges of the first and last spokes. Make sure the first and last spokes are lined up with the bottom raw edge of the background block. Make 5 blocks.

Note: The appliqué adhesive is wonderful because there are no pins, there is no slipping, and everything is in place—so flat and beautiful!

Dresden glued into place

Machine Appliqué

We love this machine appliqué technique because it does the trick and looks wonderful! It is designed to mimic hand appliqué and look invisible, not decorative.

Zigzag Appliqué Stitch

1. Use monofilament thread in the top of the machine and regular cotton piecing thread in the bobbin. Any color will work.

2. Change the machine needle to the small-size Schmetz #60 or #65.

3. Change the stitch setting to the smallest zigzag you can get (about the width of a buttonhole zigzag) so the width is equal to the length. You do not want the stitches packed too close together.

4. Drop the upper tension by 1 number on the machine settings. For example, if the upper tension is normally a #5, drop it to a #4. Make a test run through 2 layers of fabric, and make sure you do not see any bobbin thread pulling to the top. If you do, drop the tension down a little more.

5. Using this zigzag appliqué stitch, sew all 9 Dresdens into place. Make sure the stitch catches just on and off the outside edge of the Dresdens.

TIP When turning corners, it is very helpful to use the needle-down option if you have it.

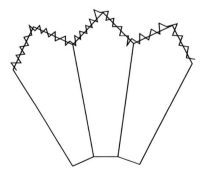

Detail of invisible appliqué stitch

Appliqué Centers

1. Make 5 vellum templates using the Dresden center pattern (next page).

2. Using a fabric glue stick, apply a small amount of glue to the edges of 1 template, and adhere it to the wrong side of the red fabric.

3. Cut out, leaving a scant ¼˝ seam allowance on the curved edge.

4. Using the fabric glue stick, apply glue to the seam allowance of the curved edge on the wrong side of the fabric (the side with vellum).

Apply fabric glue.

5. With the wrong side facing up, use an awl or Apliquick tool to fold down the seam allowance, using the edge of the vellum as a guide. This technique will produce a beautiful smooth edge. Make 5.

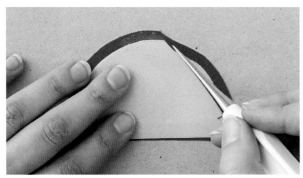

Position the seam allowance.

6. Use a few dots of the appliqué glue to affix the half-circle into place on the center of the Dresden. Make sure the bottom straight edge of the half-circle is aligned with the bottom edge of the background fabric.

7. Machine appliqué the curved edge, leaving the straight edge open.

8. Use a cotton swab dipped in a little bit of water to moisten the front and back of the curved part of the center where you applied adhesive. Wait a few minutes for the water to release the glue, then pull out the vellum from the bottom opening. Once it is dry, give the block a light press with an iron.

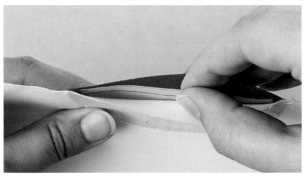

Pull out the vellum.

9. Repeat Steps 2–8 for all 5 centers.

10. Topstitch the bottom openings of the circles to the background with a straight stitch, ⅛˝ from the edge.

Optional Embroidery

Use a pencil and a small straight-edge ruler to draw a line ¼″ from the edge of the Dresden spokes. With 3 strands of red embroidery floss, stitch a small running stitch on the marked line. It is not necessary to use an embroidery hoop.

Embroidery

Stitching the Row

Stitch the Dresden blocks into a row, pressing the seams open as you go.

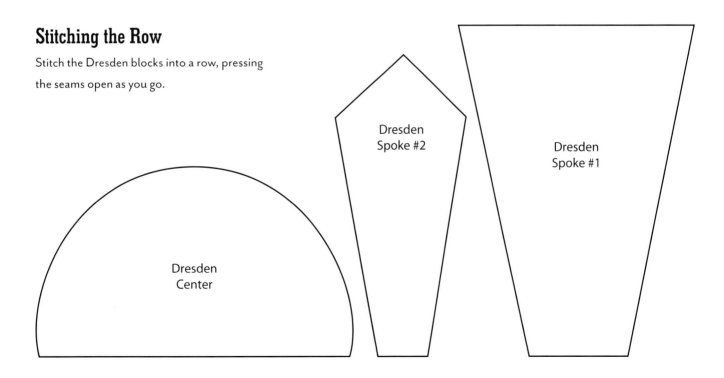

Dresden Spoke #2

Dresden Spoke #1

Dresden Center

Row 4: Pinwheels

You will master the following techniques with this row:

- Folding fabric and stitching accurately to create a relief effect

- Dealing with a lot of fabric bulk

Materials

See Fabrics (page 6) for a complete list of suggested fabrics for this quilt.

Cutting

FAT QUARTERS

- Cut 4 squares 3⅝˝ × 3⅝˝ from each of 8 fat quarters (32 total).

OFF-WHITE SOLID

- Cut 32 squares 3⅝˝ × 3⅝˝.

Preparing the Pinwheel Units

1. Press the colored squares in half diagonally, wrong sides together. Press in half diagonally again, creating a triangle that is 4 layers thick. Repeat for all 32 colored squares.

Folded triangle

2. Chainstitch together all 4 layers ⅛˝ from the raw edge.

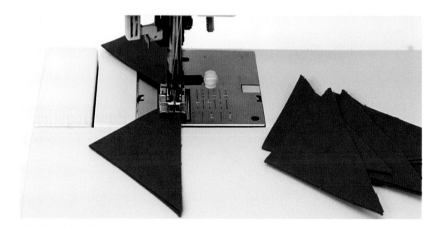

Stitch together all 4 layers.

TIP : The #90 needle will be very helpful in getting through all the layers.

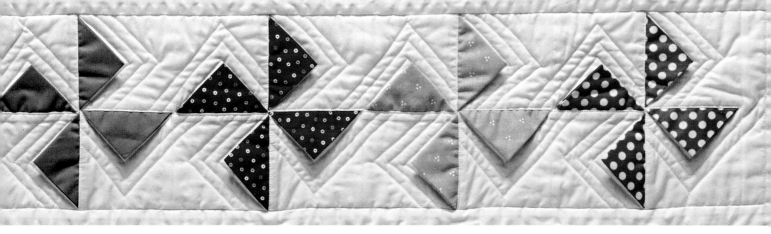

3. Fold an off-white square in half, and gently give it a little finger-pressed crease. Match up the off-white square with a triangle, and align the raw edges of the triangle with one edge of the square. Make sure the triangle point is lined up with the finger crease, and pin in place.

4. Using an ⅛″ seam, chain piece all of the triangles to the white backgrounds. This will attach the triangle to the background securely. Make 32.

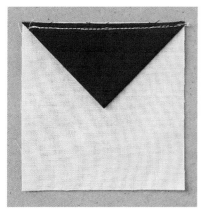

Stitched triangle

Stitching the Pinwheels

1. Arrange 4 pinwheel units into a group of matching fabrics.

2. Start with one of the groups. Using a ¼″ seam allowance, stitch 2 of the units into a pair with the correct layout, as shown. Press the

seam allowances to the off-white side; this will be the pinwheels' vertical seam. Repeat for the other matching pair.

Pinwheel pair

3. Place the right sides of the pairs together, with the seam allowances in opposing directions. Pin and stitch. Make sure the seams are butting together perfectly. Press these horizontal seams open; it will help to spread out the excess bulk. Make 8 Pinwheel blocks.

Pinwheel configuration

Putting the Row Together

Lay out the row with all 8 blocks in a pleasing color order. Mark the placement with tape, or photograph it. Stitch together all of the blocks to create the row. Press these seams open to control the bulk.

Row 5: Birds

You will master the following techniques with this row:

- Paper piecing

Materials

See Fabrics (page 6) for a complete list of suggested fabrics for this quilt.

TIP | Take a minute to study the pattern before you begin. Color placement is really important with this block. Note in particular that the shaded areas are the off-white background, and that there are two sections and then a small border at the top.

Templates

1. Trace the large and small bird patterns (pages 32 and 33) onto a sheet of template plastic. Transfer all markings on all pattern pieces, especially the background and the bird. There are 2 sections, A and B. Section A is made up of 2 subsections, A1 (which has 2 pattern pieces) and A2 (which has 6 pattern pieces). Section B is made up of 5 pattern pieces. The birds are all facing the same direction, so it is important that you do not reverse the templates.

2. Cut out all pattern pieces directly on the lines.

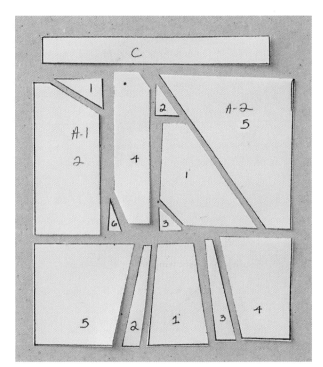

Templates for Bird block

Cutting

You will need 5 large birds and 7 small birds (you might want to make an extra bird or two, just in case). Cut each section of the pattern separately from fat quarters, starting with section B. All template pieces must be facing up, with the wrong side of the template to the wrong side of the fabric. Add a very generous ¼˝ seam allowance all the way around when cutting. Using the templates, cut 5 large and 7 small B1 pieces. This is a background piece; all background pieces will use the off-white solid.

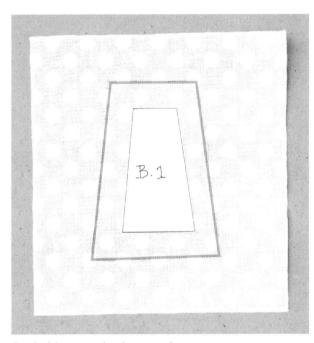

Cut the fabric using the plastic template.

Repeat for all template pattern pieces. Always cut at least 5 large and 7 small pieces of each. Remember that for all pieces marked "background," you will use the off-white solid. For all other pieces, you will use a variety of fabrics. Make sure to cut matching fabrics for the bird legs (B2 and B3).

Paper Piecing

1. Photocopy or trace 5 large and 7 small bird patterns (pages 32 and 33) onto medium-weight vellum paper.

2. Cut the sections apart, so you have separate pieces for A1, A2, B, and C.

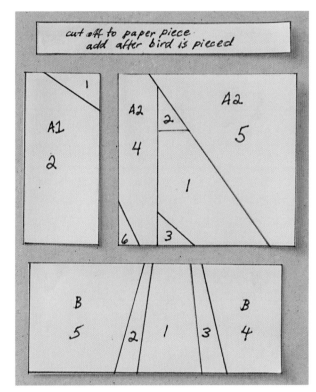

Photocopy or trace; then cut the bird pattern into separate sections.

3. You will place the fabric on the *wrong* side of the vellum and stitch on the *right* side of the vellum. The lines on the pattern are the exact stitching lines. Use a slightly smaller machine stitch than usual, and switch to the #90 machine needle (this will help the paper tear away more easily at the end). The numbers on each section indicate the stitching order.

4. Glue the wrong side of the B1 fabric in place on the wrong side of the vellum, allowing the fabric to overlap the stitching line by at least ¼″ all the way around and using just a dot of glue in the middle of the piece. (You will only glue the first fabric piece on each section.) Then place the fabric for B2 on top, right sides together. Match the raw edges with a ¼″ seam allowance beyond the stitching line between B1 and B2. Pin in place.

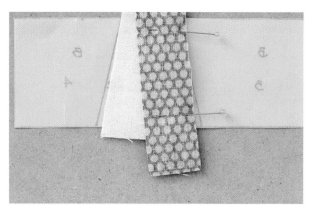

B1 and B2 fabric pieces pinned in place to wrong side of vellum

5. Turn the vellum over to the right side, and stitch on the line between B1 and B2, starting ¼″ before the beginning of the paper and ending ¼″ beyond.

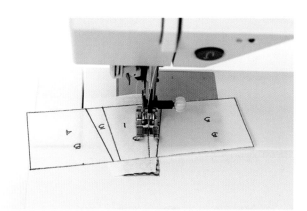

Stitch on the line between B1 and B2.

6. Fold piece B2 open, and make sure it completely covers section B2 on the paper, with at least an extra ¼″ for the next seam allowance and ¼″ hanging over the vellum at the top and bottom. Using a small pair of scissors, eyeball a ¼″ seam allowance on the seam already sewn, and trim any excess beyond it.

Trim the seam allowance to ¼″.

TIP ┊ For very small pieces, like B2, B3, A2-2, A2-3, and A2-6, trim the seam allowance a little bit smaller than ¼″.

7. Press the seamline flat.

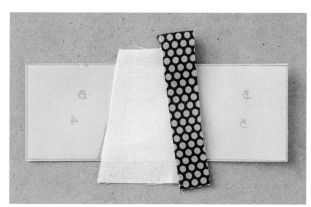

Press.

---

8. Repeat Steps 1–7 until you have finished sections B, A1, and A2 for all 12 bird blocks. For section C, which is just a single strip, attach the fabric to the vellum with a couple of dots of fabric glue to hold it while you trim. Trim around all sections on all sides with a ¼″ seam allowance beyond the outside line of the pattern. Do not remove the vellum yet.

Stitching Together the Paper-Pieced Sections

1. Place sections A1 and A2 right sides together. Pin and stitch together. Press open all seam allowances between the sections.

2. Stitch section B to A as above, and then stitch section C to the unit. Repeat Steps 1 and 2 for all 12 Bird blocks.

3. Tear away the vellum from all the Bird blocks. Pull the fabric slightly to separate the paper from the seam; then fold the vellum on the seamline, and completely tear it away.

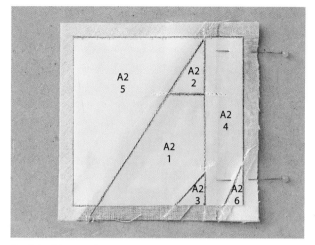

Pin right sides together.

Putting Together the Row

1. Hand stitch a bead onto each Bird block for the eye.

2. Stitch together 12 birds into a row, following our layout or your own arrangement.

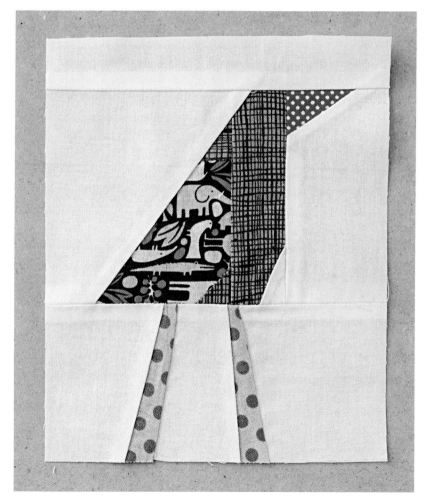

Paper-pieced bird

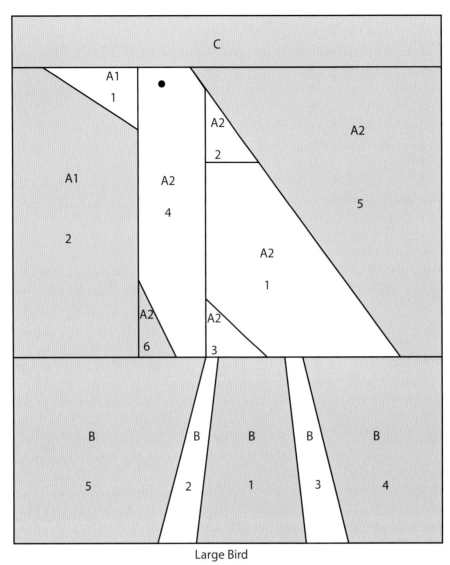

Large Bird

Shaded areas are background fabric

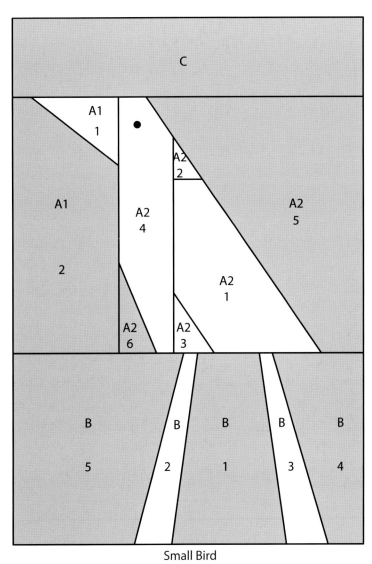

Small Bird

Shaded areas are background fabric

Row 6: Posy Flowers

You will master the following techniques with this row:

- Careful color placement for paper piecing

Materials

See Fabrics (page 6) for a complete list of suggested fabrics for this quilt.

TIP When choosing colors, remember that the row will be far more vibrant if you use a full range of light to dark fabrics with lots of contrast. Don't be afraid of using black.

Templates

You only need templates for the stem/leaf sections. Trace the stem/leaf section of the pattern (page 39) onto template plastic. This includes sections A, B, and C (all numbers).

Cut out all pattern pieces directly on the lines, and throw away section C (you will not need a template for this).

Cutting

TIP To give your flowers a beautiful scrappy look, cut every piece in a variety of fabrics. For example, when cutting the flower stems, use as many different greens as possible.

STEM/LEAF SECTIONS

TIP Because there are so many angles on these leaves, you must add a 3/8″ seam allowance while cutting.

Use the templates to cut out all the stem/leaf fabric pieces on the bottom half of the flowers for both sections A and B. *Pay careful attention to which ones are the off-white background pieces.*

- Cut pieces for all 7 large flowers and all 9 small flowers.

TIP Since you are cutting many different section pieces in many different fabrics for these flowers, we strongly suggest that you keep all the pieces for each flower together in a clearly labeled pile.

- Cut 7 strips 1″ × 6″ for the large flower stems (section C).

- Cut 9 strips 3/4″ × 3½″ for the small flower stems (section C).

FLOWERS (*NO TEMPLATES*)

TIP This row looks best if it is really scrappy. Make sure you also cut the flower pieces in a variety of colors and prints. For example, when you cut 9 squares for the small flower center, cut from several different fabrics.

Fat quarters

- Cut 1½″ × LOG strips from a variety of colors for the large flower petals (2 through 4).

- Cut 1¼″ × LOG strips from a variety of colors for the small flower petals (2 through 4).

- Cut 7 squares 1¾″ × 1¾″ for the large flower centers (1).

- Cut 9 squares 1¼″ × 1¼″ for the small flower centers (1).

OFF-WHITE SOLID

- Cut 2 strips 1¼″ × WOF for the large flower background (5); you'll need about 70″ total.

- Cut 1 strip 1″ × WOF for the small flower background (5); you'll need about 41″ total.

- Cut 9 rectangles 3″ × 3¾″. These will be stitched at the top of the small flowers so they fit into the row.

- Cut 14 squares 2″ × 2″; then cut them in half diagonally to create 28 corner triangles for the large flowers (6).

- Cut 18 squares 1¾″ × 1¾″; then cut them in half diagonally to create 36 corner triangles for the small flowers (6).

Paper Piecing

1. Photocopy or trace the large and small flower patterns onto vellum paper, making sure to transfer all numbers and markings. You need 7 large flower templates and 9 small flower templates. It is helpful to make an extra template of each in case of mistakes.

2. Cut apart the vellum flowers by section, creating a flower top and sections A, B, and C.

3. Paper piece sections A and B as you did in Row 5: Birds, Paper Piecing (page 29).

> **TIP** Because sections A and B of the leaves have so many angles, it can be difficult to judge where to place the fabric pieces prior to stitching. We suggest you use an extra ⅛″ seam allowance to help with this problem. Prior to pinning the fabric piece down, fold the seam allowance under and hold the piece in place; then check if it is correct.

4. Complete all sections A and B for all flowers.

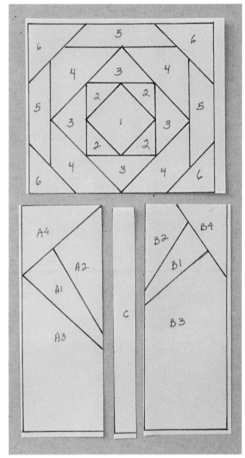

Cut apart vellum flower sections.

5. Stitch together the A and B sections for all flowers by joining a C stem strip in the middle. Make sure to use the correct size of strips depending on whether it is a large or small flower. Trim the stem/leaf section, leaving a ¼″ seam allowance all the way around.

Completed stem/leaf section

6. Turn the vellum piece for the top of the flower to the wrong side. Using a fabric glue stick, glue the fabric for center square 1 into place with a dot of glue (remember to only glue down the first piece to a section). From this point forward, make sure there is a ¼″ seam allowance outside the stitch line on all sides when attaching fabrics.

7. Cut a piece of a correct-size strip (depending on if you are starting with a large or small flower) for 1 of the section 2s, and pin it right sides together on top of the center piece 1. The piece should be long enough to extend at least ¼″ beyond each side of the line between sections 1 and 2.

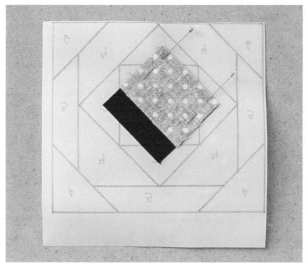

Pin a piece 2 fabric on top of piece 1.

8. Repeat Step 7 for the opposing piece 2.

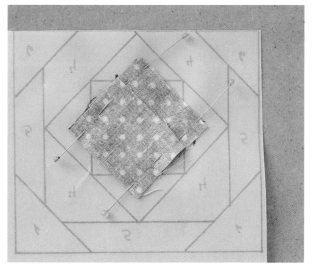

Repeat for the opposing piece 2.

9. Stitch on the lines for both of the piece 2s. Trim both seam allowances down to about ¼˝ on the large flowers and ⅛˝ on the small ones. (There is no need to use a ruler; just gauge the measurement roughly.) Press.

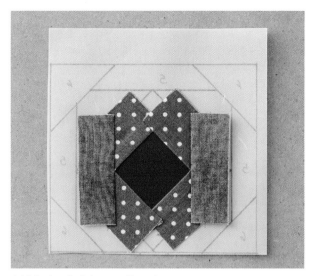

Add the first 2 of the piece 3s and press.

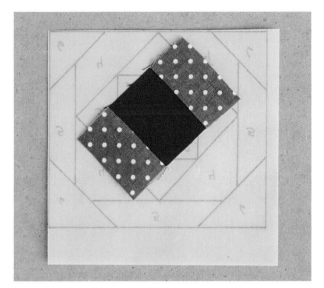

Stitch, trim down the seam allowances, and press.

10. Repeat this process with the other 2 opposing piece 2s and all of the following numbers through 5 for all of the flower tops.

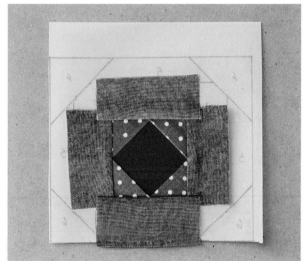

Add the remaining piece 3s and press.

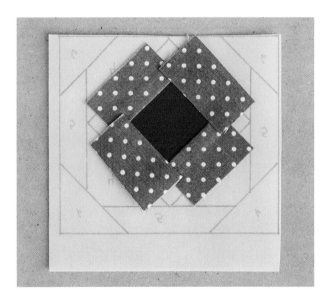

All 4 of the piece 2s have been stitched and pressed.

Add the piece 4s and press.

11. Add the piece 5s using background fabric, and then stitch the correct-size triangles for the corner 6s in the same manner on all of the blocks.

Stitch the corner triangle 6s.

At this point, you should have all of the stem/leaf and flower sections completely paper pieced for both sizes and trimmed with a ¼˝ seam allowance.

12. Match the 2 block sections, right sides together, and stitch with a ¼˝ seam allowance to complete the block. Press the seam open.

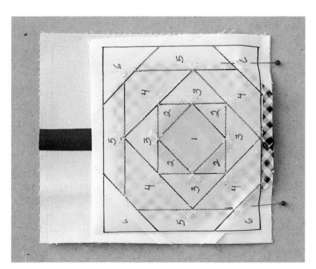

Stitch together the block halves.

13. Stitch an off-white 3˝ × 3¾˝ rectangle to the top of every Small Flower block. Press the seam allowances toward the plain block.

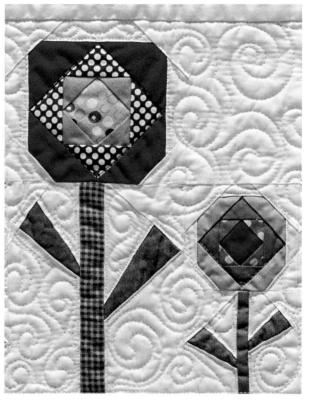

Complete flower blocks

Putting Together the Row

Stitch together all the flowers in a row. Press the seams open.

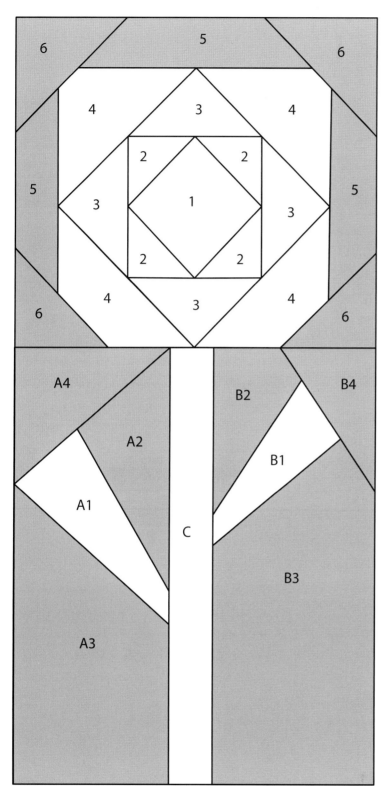

Shaded areas are background fabric.

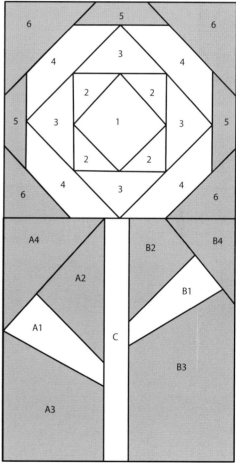

Shaded areas are background fabric.

Row 7: Dancing Squares

You will master the following techniques with this row:

- Constructing on-point squares
- Marking and stitching on a diagonal
- Managing a bias raw edge

Materials

See Fabrics (page 6) for a complete list of suggested fabrics for this quilt.

Cutting

ORANGE DOT

- Cut 7 squares 3⅝″ × 3⅝″.

TEAL SOLID

- Cut 7 squares 3⅝″ × 3⅝″.

PINK PRINT

- Cut 15 squares 3¾″ × 3¾″; then cut them in half diagonally, creating 30 setting triangles.

Marking Diagonals

1. Using a short ruler and mechanical pencil, draw a diagonal line from corner to corner on all the teal squares.

2. Draw a line ¼″ on each side of the first line. The centerline is the cutting line, and the lines on each side are the stitching lines.

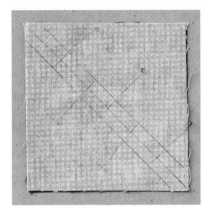

Draw a line ¼″ on each side of the first line.

Stitching

1. Place all the orange and teal squares in pairs, right sides together, with the drawn lines going the same direction.

2. Stitch directly on the stitch lines.

3. Cut through both layers of fabric on the center cutting line. You should now have 14 half-square

triangle blocks. (You will use 13; the other is extra.)

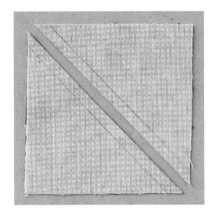

Stitch; then cut on the centerline.

4. Press all seam allowances toward the orange fabric. Trim each unit to 3¼″ square if necessary.

Half-square triangles

TIP | Remember, you are working on the bias, and it will stretch. Take extra care in pressing.

Setting Triangles

1. Pin and stitch a pink setting triangle to the right side of all 13 half-square triangles. Alternate the orange and teal as the color on the right. (Because you have an uneven number of half-square triangles, one color will be on the right an additional time.) Pay close attention to the orientation of the triangles.

Half-square triangle unit

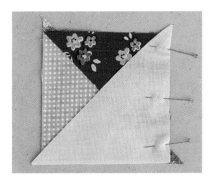

Pin and stitch a setting triangle to the right side.

2. Stitch the second setting triangle to the left of all the units. Press the seam allowances toward the pink print.

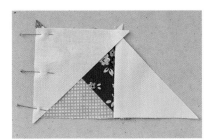

Stitch a second setting triangle to the left.

Putting Together the Row

1. Stitch together the half-square triangle units into pairs, making sure to alternate the colors on top. There will be an extra; set it aside until the end.

Stitch together half-square triangle units into pairs.

2. Stitch the pairs into a row.

3. You should have 4 extra pink print setting triangles. Stitch 2 pink print setting triangles together, and add a pair to each end of the row, as shown.

Add 2 setting triangles to the end of the row on both sides.

Row 8: Spring Garden

You will master the following techniques with this row:

- Organization while piecing
- Working with small pieces

Materials

See Fabrics (page 6) for a complete list of suggested fabrics for this quilt.

Cutting

TIP As you cut, we suggest you label each pile, which flower (A or B) it is for, and its measurement. Push a pin through the label and the entire stack to keep it together, or place it in a small plastic bag. In this block, there are many fabric cuts that look similar in size and are from the same fabric, so labeling will help you avoid mistakes.

FLOWER BLOCK A

Light blue print

- Cut 12 rectangles 1½˝ × 2½˝.
- Cut 18 squares 1⅞˝ × 1⅞˝.
- Cut 12 squares 1½˝ × 1½˝.

Red print

- Cut 12 rectangles 1½˝ × 2½˝.
- Cut 48 squares 1½˝ × 1½˝.
- Cut 24 squares 1˝ × 1˝.

Pink print

- Cut 12 rectangles 1½˝ × 2½˝.
- Cut 24 squares 1˝ × 1˝.

Yellow solid

- Cut 12 rectangles 1½˝ × 2½˝.

Green print

- Cut 3 squares 2½˝ × 2½˝.

Off-white solid

- Cut 7 strips 1⅛˝ × 8½˝ for vertical sashing that will be between each flower block, as well as on the outside edges.
- Cut 18 squares 1⅞˝ × 1⅞˝.
- Cut 12 squares 1½˝ × 1½˝.
- Cut 12 squares 1˝ × 1˝.

FLOWER BLOCK B

Red print

- Cut 12 rectangles 1½˝ × 2½˝.

- Cut 18 squares 1⅞˝ × 1⅞˝.

- Cut 12 squares 1½˝ × 1½˝.

Light blue print

- Cut 12 rectangles 1½˝ × 2½˝.

- Cut 48 squares 1½˝ × 1½˝.

- Cut 24 squares 1˝ × 1˝.

Yellow solid

- Cut 12 rectangles 1½˝ × 2½˝.

- Cut 24 squares 1˝ × 1˝.

Pink print

- Cut 12 rectangles 1½˝ × 2½˝.

Green print

- Cut 3 squares 2½˝ × 2½˝.

Off-white solid

- Cut 18 squares 1⅞˝ × 1⅞˝.

- Cut 12 squares 1½˝ × 1½˝.

- Cut 12 squares 1˝ × 1˝.

> **TIP** Assemble the blocks one at a time. Complete all A flowers first, followed by all B flowers. There are three of each type of flower, making a total of six flowers in the row. It can be very confusing to work on the different blocks at the same time.

A

B

Constructing Tiny Units

You will need to construct three different block pieces that are part of both the A and B flowers, just in different color combos. Use the following instructions to create the correct number you need for each block.

	Unit 1 half-square triangles:	Unit 2 quarter-square triangles:	Unit 3 rectangle with corners:	Unit 4 Snowball block:
Flower A (3):	Blue/white—make 12.	Large red/small blue triangles—make 24 using Unit 1s.	Pink with red corners—make 12.	Green center with white corners—make 3.
			Yellow with pink corners—make 12.	
Flower B (3):	Red/white—make 12.	Large blue/small red triangles—make 24 using Unit 1s.	Yellow with blue corners—make 12.	Green center with white corners—make 3.
			Pink with yellow corners—make 12.	

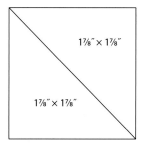

Unit 1: half-square triangle

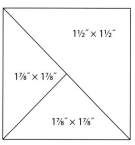

Unit 2: quarter-square triangle

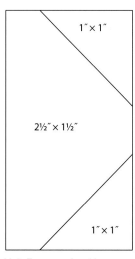

Unit 3: rectangle with corners

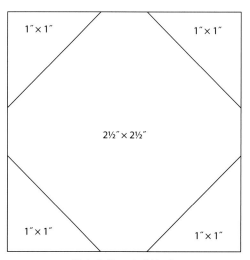

Unit 4: Snowball block

Tiny Unit 1

1. Using the correct fabrics, place 2 different 1⅞" × 1⅞" squares right sides together. Draw a diagonal line from corner to corner.

2. Draw a line a scant ¼" on each side of the first line. The centerline is the cutting line, and the lines on each side are the stitching lines.

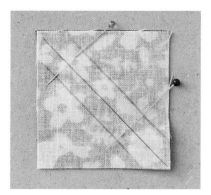

Draw stitching and cutting lines.

3. Stitch directly on the stitching lines.

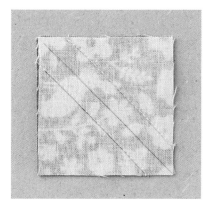

Stitch on the stitching lines.

4. Cut from corner to corner on the cutting line. You will always have a yield of 2 at a time. Press the seam allowance toward the darker fabric. The 2 half-square triangle units should measure 1½" × 1½" at this point. Make 12 units for each flower;

8 will be used to make the quarter-square triangles.

Tiny Unit 1

Tiny Unit 2

1. Use Tiny Unit 1 with the fabrics for Unit 2.

2. Place a half-square triangle block with a 1½" × 1½" square, right sides together. Draw a pencil line down the middle diagonally, as shown. (This line will cross the stitching line of the half-square triangle Unit 1.)

Pin right sides together, and draw a diagonal line.

3. Stitch along the drawn line.

4. You are going to trim the seam allowance, but you don't want to trim them all the same! Open up each unit before trimming, and press toward the larger triangle so that half the units have the small off-white triangle to the lower left of the large triangle and the others have the small off-white triangle to the lower right of the small triangle. Then trim the seam allowance ¼" from the stitching line.

Press the large triangles for 2 configurations of the small triangles.

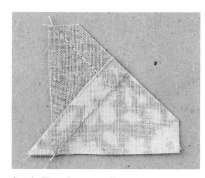

Stitch. Trim the seam allowance.

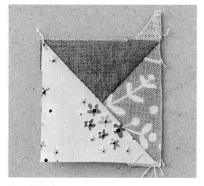

Tiny Unit 2

Tiny Unit 3

1. Using the fabrics for Unit 3, place a 1˝ × 1˝ square in a top corner of a 1½˝ × 2½˝ rectangle, right sides together. Line up the outside raw edges perfectly. Draw a diagonal line, as shown, for the stitch line.

2. Stitch on the drawn line, trim off any excess over a ¼˝ seam allowance, and press the seams toward the darker fabric.

3. Repeat Steps 1 and 2 on the other end of the same long side of the rectangle. Make 8 in 2 colorways for each flower.

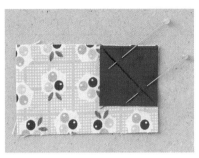

Place a 1˝ × 1˝ square in a corner of a 1½˝ × 2½˝ rectangle. Draw a diagonal stitch line.

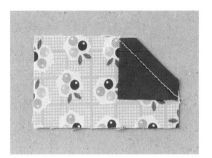

Stitch. Trim the seam allowance.

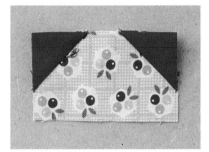

Tiny Unit 3

Tiny Unit 4

1. Place a 1˝ × 1˝ off-white square in each corner of a 2½˝ × 2½˝ green square, right sides together. Line up the outside raw edges perfectly. Draw a diagonal line on each off-white square, as shown, for the stitch line.

2. Stitch on the drawn lines, trim off any excess over a ¼˝ seam allowance, and press the seams toward the darker fabric.

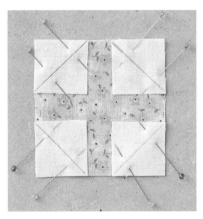

1˝ squares placed right sides together on a 2½˝ square with lines drawn diagonally

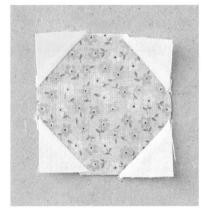

Tiny Unit 4

Putting Together Flower Blocks

1. Stitch together the tiny units in horizontal rows, referring to the diagrams (below) for placement.

Note: There are seven rows. The center row (row four) is composed of only rectangles and the larger center square, so it will be twice as high as all the other rows.

----

2. Press the seam allowances on all even-numbered rows to the right and on all odd-numbered rows to the left, so you can butt the seams accurately when you sew together the rows.

> **TIP** ┆ As you complete each row, label it with a row number and mark the right-hand side so that you do not end up flipping the row upside down. This extra step will save you a great deal of time and make the process go more smoothly.

3. Stitch together all 7 rows to create a finished Flower block.

> **TIP** ┆ Remember to stitch all A blocks first and then all B blocks. We promise it will make life a lot easier.

4. Using this method, complete the other Flower blocks for a total of 6 finished Flower blocks (3 each of A and B) that should each measure 8½˝ × 8½˝.

Putting Together the Row

Stitch together the blocks, alternating A and B with a 1⅛˝ × 8½˝ sashing strip between the blocks and on the outside edges.

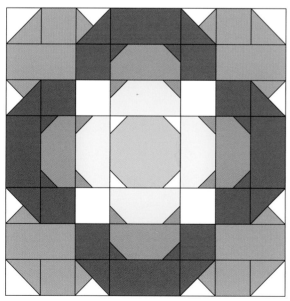

Flower block A

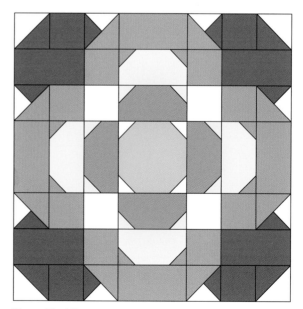

Flower block B

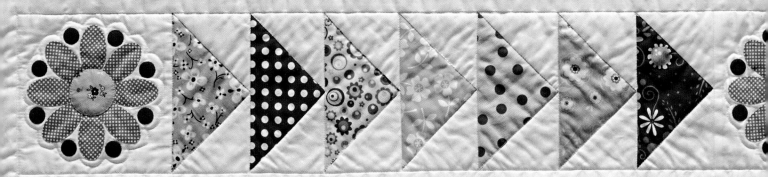

Row 9: Flying Geese

You will master the following techniques with this row:

- Stitching Flying Geese
- Machine appliqué
- Perfect appliqué circles

Materials

See Fabrics (page 6) for a complete list of suggested fabrics for this quilt.

Cutting

FAT QUARTERS

- Cut 14 rectangles 3˝ × 5½˝ for the Flying Geese, 2 each from 7 different fat quarters.

OFF-WHITE SOLID

- Cut 3 strips 3˝ × WOF; then cut them into 28 squares 3˝ × 3˝ for the Flying Geese.

- Cut 3 squares 5½˝ × 5½˝ for the flower backgrounds.

Stitching Flying Geese

1. Lightly draw a diagonal line from one corner to the opposite corner on the wrong side of 2 squares.

2. With right sides together, place a square on one end of the rectangle. Sew directly on the line, trim the seam allowance to ¼˝, and press toward the triangle.

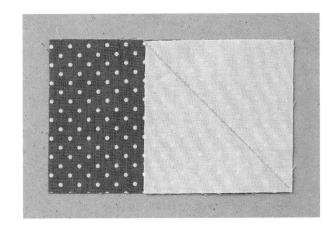

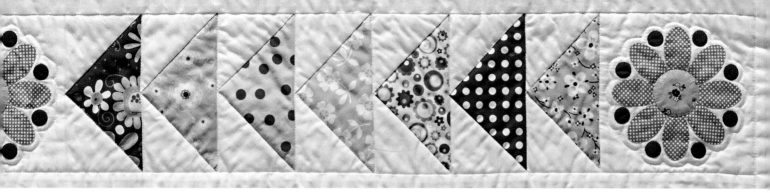

3. With right sides together, place the other square on the other end of the rectangle. Sew directly on the line, trim the seam allowance to ¼˝, and press toward the triangle.

Finished Flying Geese unit

Machine Appliqué

Appliqué Flowers

1. Trace 24 flower petals from the appliqué pattern (page 53) onto freezer paper (the non-shiny paper side) or Apliquick interfacing. Cut them out exactly on the line.

2. Press the freezer-paper or interfacing petals to the wrong side of the blue fabric, leaving at least ¾˝ between each petal.

3. Cut out each petal, adding a scant ¼˝ seam allowance.

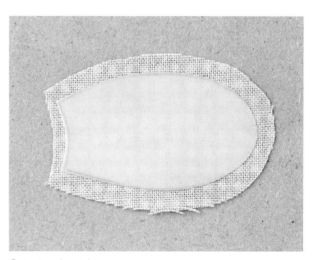

Cut out each petal.

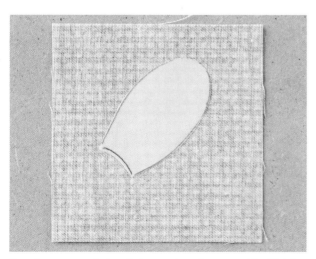

Press freezer-paper or interfacing petals to the wrong side of fabric.

4. Using a fabric glue stick on the wrong side of the fabric, smear a thin coat of glue on the seam allowance all the way around the curved edges of the petal but not on the straight edge. Let it sit for a minute to allow the adhesive to get tacky.

Add glue on seam allowance.

5. Holding an awl as you would a pencil, fold in the seam allowance. The bottom of the petal should remain a raw edge, so when the center circle is placed, there will not be an ugly bump.

Position the seam allowance with an awl.

The bottom of the petal should remain a raw edge.

6. Create center marks in the 3 squares 5½˝ × 5½˝ for the flower backgrounds by finger-pressing them in half both horizontally and vertically.

7. Using appliqué adhesive, adhere the petals to the background so they are ready to be stitched into place. Use the center mark for accurate placement. There are 8 petals on each flower. Use the appliqué placement diagram (page 53).

8. Using the zigzag appliqué stitch from Row 3: Dresden, Zigzag Appliqué Stitch (page 23), stitch down all of the flower petals along the curved edges.

9. Spritz the back side of the block with a little water; then pull the freezer paper softly with tweezers or hemostats, removing it through the unsewn straight end of each petal. If you chose to use interfacing, skip this step.

Appliqué Circles

1. Using the appliqué patterns (page 53), trace and cut 3 flower center templates and 24 small circle templates from vellum paper.

> TIP : If you scrapbook and have 1⅝″ and ½″ circle punches, you can use them to speed up this process.

2. Using a fabric glue stick, adhere the small circles to the wrong side of the red fabric and the large circles to the wrong side of the pink fabric.

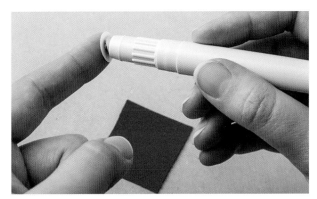

Glue the circles to the wrong side of the fabric.

3. Cut out a square shape around the circle.

Cut a square shape.

4. Using light-colored quilting thread, hand stitch a tiny running stitch around the circle a scant ⅛″ from the edge of the vellum, with the wrong side facing you. Bring the needle to the right side with the last stitch.

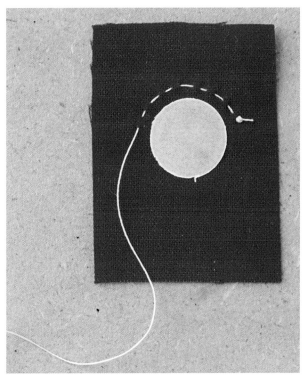

Stitch a tiny running stitch around the circle.

5. Trim the excess fabric in a circle to ⅛″ from the stitching line.

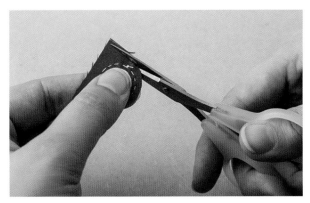

Trim the excess fabric to ⅛″ from the stitching line.

6. Pull the thread tight, and do a little backstitch to hold the hand stitching in place. Cut the thread.

Pull the thread tight.

Finished circle

7. Repeat Steps 3–6 on all of the large and small circles.

8. Using white appliqué adhesive, adhere all the circles in the appropriate spot on the flower background. Using the zigzag appliqué stitch, stitch down the circles. The vellum does not need to be removed; it will eventually wash away.

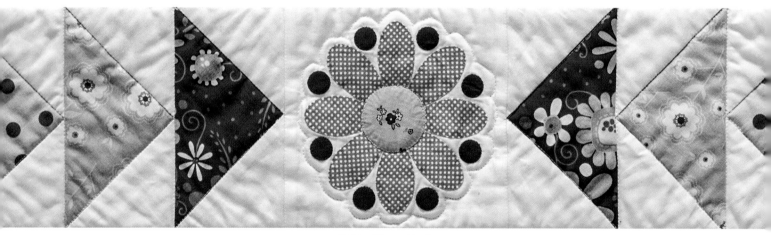

Finished flower block

Putting Together the Row

Using the row image (pages 48 and 49) for the layout, stitch together the Flying Geese and Flower blocks.

Appliqué placement

Small Circle
Make 8.

Flower Petal
Make 8.

Flower Center
Make 1.

Row 10: French Braid

You will master the following techniques with this row:

- Stitching on a diagonal
- Accurate cutting of the row after construction

Materials

See Fabrics (page 6) for a complete list of suggested fabrics for this quilt.

Cutting

FAT QUARTERS

- Cut 4 strips 1¼˝ × 5˝ from each of 25 different fat quarters.

- Cut 1 square 3¾˝ × 3¾˝ from 2 additional fat quarters; then cut them in half diagonally. You will only use 1 triangle of each fabric.

- Cut 1 square 4˝ × 4˝ from another fat quarter; then cut it in half diagonally. You will only use 1 triangle.

Stitching

1. Pin 1 strip 1¼˝ × 5˝ to the side of the 4˝ × 4˝ triangle, lining up the ends.

2. Stitch. Press the seam allowance toward the triangle.

Large triangle plus a strip

Stitch and press.

3. Pin the next strip to the opposite side of the triangle, lining up the short end with the long side of the previous strip. Stitch. Press the seam allowances—and all seam allowances from this point on—toward the strip you just stitched.

Pin next strip. Stitch.

Press toward the newest strip.

4. Repeat Step 3 with all the strips.

Continue adding strips.

Putting Together the Row

After all the strips are used, pin and stitch the 2 small triangles to either side, one at a time. The triangles will square up the ends of the row.

Pin and stitch the small triangles.

Cutting the Row to the Correct Height

Note: For consistency, we will use "width" of the quilt to mean from side to side and "length" of the quilt to mean from top to bottom. "Width" of the row means the long measurement from side to side. The short dimension of the row is the "height."

This is the only row in the quilt where you have to trim down the height to ensure the correct shape.

1. Start with the tip of the first triangle, and imagine an invisible line along all the points extending out from that tip. These points are the center of the row. Once you have identified this centerline, lay a ruler down and cut

2½˝ from the line, making sure you're lined up with all the center points. Use the ruler to cut across the row, moving the ruler along as you go. (The ruler is not long enough to allow you to trim the whole length at once.)

Cut 2½˝ from the centerline.

2. Turn the row around, and repeat the same process on the other side of the centerline, trimming 2½˝ from the centerline across the center points. The finished Row 10 should measure 5˝ × your original row's width that you marked with masking tape (see Oops! Adjusting the Row Measurement, page 15).

Row 11: Happy Trails

Appliqué

This entire row is appliqué. Don't let it scare you! It can be very fun and will make you an expert in the end. But also don't feel guilty about removing some of our images to make the row easier, if you would like. We suggest using the machine appliqué techniques from Row 9: Flying Geese, Machine Appliqué (page 49) throughout, with a little bit of reverse appliqué where needed. We love the look of these methods, as the edges will be turned under and have the appearance of handwork. But if you prefer, you could use fusible web (like HeatnBond Lite), leave the edges raw, and stitch everything down to make it super simple. Do what works best for you!

Reverse Appliqué Pond

Reverse appliqué is a wonderful technique that provides beautiful depth in fabrics and is great for small detail work. The technique is not used as often as it should be because many quilters think it's difficult. Really, it's quite simple once you know how. We are going to teach you how to use reverse appliqué to attach the pond for this row. You may decide to use it for the other appliqués in this row—it's up to you. Sometimes, using a variety of appliqué techniques can make a quilt more interesting and make appliquéing different shapes easier. We think this is one of the secrets to the beautiful appliqué results we achieve in our quilts.

1. Use the grass pattern (pullout page P2) to make a template. You will need to trace the 3 sections onto sheets of paper and tape them together. Line up the bottom edge of the green fabric strip with the bottom line of the pattern, and draw the top wavy line for the grass onto the right side of the green fabric. Flip the template over, and draw the same line on the back of the green grass fabric. It should follow the same path as the line you just traced on the front. *Do not cut it out yet.*

You will master the following techniques with this row:

- Machine appliqué
- Reverse appliqué

Materials

See Fabrics (page 6) for a complete list of suggested fabrics for this quilt.

Use scraps from various fat quarters for the appliqué.

Cutting

OFF-WHITE SOLID

- See Cutting Borders, Sashing, and Long Rows (page 13). This was already cut and set aside.

GREEN

- See Cutting Borders, Sashing, and Long Rows (page 13). This was already cut and set aside.

Note: You will cut all of the appliqué pieces as you stitch.

Placement for additional vine

2. Make a vellum template of the pond (pattern pullout page P2) exactly as is—do not add any seam allowance, and cut it out exactly on the line.

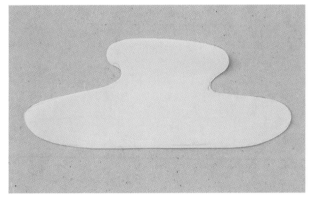

Vellum pond template

3. Cut a piece of freezer paper that is about 1˝ larger all around than the pond. Press the shiny side down on the wrong side of a piece of light blue fabric for the pond, and cut out around the freezer paper exactly (no seam allowance).

Freezer paper ironed to pond fabric

4. Trace the vellum pond template onto the right side of the green grass fabric.

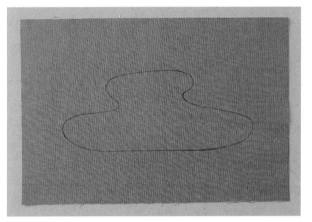

Trace the vellum pond template onto the green grass fabric.

5. Place the right side of the light blue fabric to the wrong side of the green grass fabric, centering it directly behind the pond placement line. Hand baste ⅜˝ outside the line all around, joining both layers of fabric and the freezer paper.

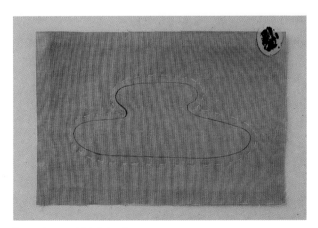

Baste the pond fabric in place.

6. With a pair of very small embroidery scissors, cut a scant ¼" inside the pond placement line, removing only the grass fabric and exposing the blue pond fabric. On all inside curves, cut a series of ease clips spaced ⅛" apart.

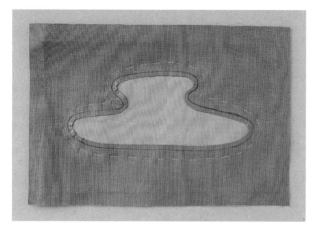

Cut out the grass fabric, exposing the blue pond.

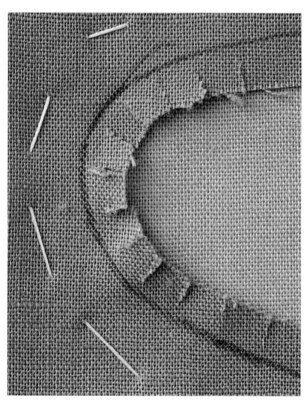

Ease clips

7. Using a fabric glue stick, apply glue on the scant ¼" seam allowance, and use an awl to sweep the seam allowance under to the wrong side. (Use your pencil line as a guide.) Stitch the folded edge into place with matching or clear monofilament thread.

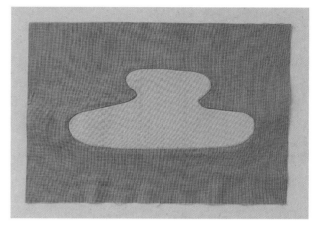

Turn under the seam allowance. Stitch.

8. Carefully trim the extra light-blue pond fabric on the back side ¼" from the appliqué stitching line.

9. Remove the basting stitches and freezer paper. Spritz the back of the fabric lightly with water to release the adhesive. Hemostats or tweezers work great to grab the freezer paper and pull it away from the fabric.

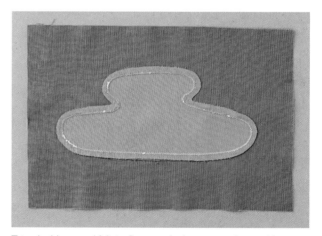

Trim the blue pond fabric. Remove the basting stitches and freezer paper.

Machine Appliqué

1. Using the grass template you prepared, flip it over, and trace and cut out the grass from the non-shiny side of the Apliquick or a similar interfacing. Make sure to cut it exactly (no seam allowance).

2. Position the interfacing shiny side to the wrong side of the grass fabric, making sure you have at least a ¼˝ seam allowance around the 3 straight edges. Press in place. *Make sure to accurately line up the interfacing's top wavy edge with the traced line from before.*

3. Trim the top wavy edge with a ¼˝ seam allowance beyond the interfacing edge. Snip ease clips on all of the inside curves.

4. Using a fabric glue stick and with the wrong side of fabric facing you, apply glue to the seam allowance and the top about 3˝–6˝ at a time. (The adhesive sets up very quickly, and this edge is very long, so you are going to keep applying glue as you are working along.) Turn the edge under using an awl or Apliquick tool and the same method from the flowers in Row 9: Flying Geese, Appliqué Flowers (page 49).

5. Using appliqué basting glue, adhere the grass into place on the off-white background piece, lining up the bottom corners and the sides of both the green and white pieces.

6. Continue using the machine appliqué instructions from Row 9: Flying Geese, Machine Appliqué, Steps 1–5 and Step 7 (pages 49 and 50) to trace, cut, turn edges under, and adhere all of the appliqué pieces onto the background. Use the row image (pages 56 and 57) for placement. It is best to appliqué in an assembly-line method, meaning that you will stitch all the pieces at once after they are prepared and adhered into place. Use the zigzag appliqué stitch from Row 3: Dresden, Zigzag Appliqué Stitch (page 23) to stitch all of the appliqué pieces into place.

Embroidery Detail

A lot of small details on this row are added with embroidery stitches because they are too tiny to appliqué. All embroidery stitches are done with 2 or 3 strands of floss, using a stem stitch or backstitch and French knots for details on flowers, mushrooms, and animal eyes. (See Simple Embroidery Stitches, page 15.) Refer to the row photo (pages 56 and 57) for placement and the embroidery details photo (below) for details.

Have fun with this—use your own ideas for details! If embroidery is not your thing, you can replace the stitches with little buttons and trims that save time and are just as fun. These details are optional; you may leave them off if you wish.

Embroidery details

Putting Together the Row

To finish this row, you only need to trim it. Square up the row by cutting off extra fabric from the top and bottom without getting too close to any of the appliqué pieces. (You will need a ¼˝ seam allowance to stitch together the rows.) If possible, trim about 1˝; you can trim as little as ¼˝ to square up the row. Trim the width according to your marked tape measurement (see Oops! Adjusting the Row Measurement, page 15).

Row 11 is finished! Can you believe it?! Now you are ready to put everything together.

Putting It All Together

Beautiful border and binding with rickrack detail

You will master the following techniques as you finish the quilt:

- Measuring the quilt to add accurate borders
- Layering, basting, and binding the quilt
- Adding rickrack into binding

Materials

See Fabrics (page 6) for a complete list of suggested fabrics for this quilt.

Cutting

BLUE

- Cut 4 strips 2½″ × LOG. (You will cut this further as you attach the border strips.)

BINDING

- Cut bias strips 2½″ wide to equal a total of 290″ long.

1. Fold the binding fabric up to form 1 large triangle with a strip "left over" at one side.

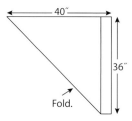

2. Trim off about ¼″ along the folded edge of the triangle to form the base for your bias strips.

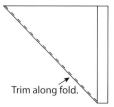

3. Then cut strips 2½″ wide parallel to the bias line, including the "left-over" fabric. You will get 2 strips from each cut.

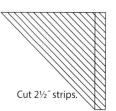

Sashing

Using the tape method in Oops! Adjusting the Row Measurement (page 15), make sure all 11 of the rows are the same width.

1. Fold Row 9 in half, lining up the raw edges of the sides.

2. Place pins on the fold at the top and bottom edges and in the middle; then open the row back up and lay it flat. Repeat this same process with 2 of the off-white sashing strips.

3. Loosely pin together the 2 sashing strips and lay them on top of the first row, centering it. Make scissor nicks (small cuts within the seam allowances) on the top and bottom edges through all fabrics (both sashings and the first row) ⅛″ deep on both sides of the center fold. Through both of the sashing strips *only*, make scissor nicks on the top and bottom at both of the side raw edges of the first row.

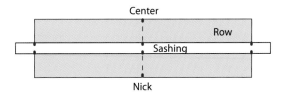

4. Remove the pins, and line up one of these sashing strips with one long edge of the row. Pin, making sure to match the nicks at the center and to line up both nicks on the right side with the raw edge of the row, making sure it lines up in a perfect right (90°) angle. Then match up the nicks on the left side. Evenly pin the long edges into place.

> **TIP** | If there is any extra fullness, spread it evenly throughout.

5. Stitch in place; then press the seam toward the sashing.

> **TIP** | Always press the seams toward the sashing or borders. If you press toward a row, the seam may appear crooked because there are so many intersecting seams.

> **Note:** Because all of the sashing strips and borders are cut on the LOG, there will be no stretching and the quilt will be perfectly square.

6. Use this method for the rest of the sashing strips until the quilt center is entirely put together. Stitch the rows together in pairs, then in groups of four, and so on until the quilt center is complete. Refer to the quilt assembly diagram (below).

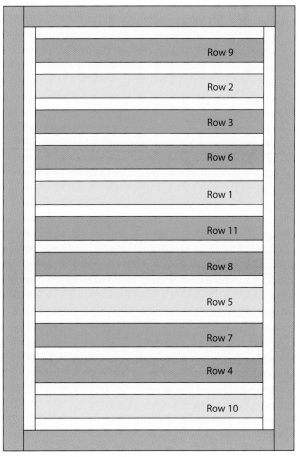

Quilt assembly (not to scale)

Borders

The borders consist of small off-white inner borders and larger blue outer borders. Attach all of the borders using the method described in Sashing, Steps 1–5 (page 61). Always start with the top and bottom borders, and then add both sides. The opposite borders of the quilt can be pinned together lengthwise and treated as one for measurement and marking.

Finishing

1. Cut the backing fabric in half from selvage to selvage, and trim off the selvages. Place the pieces with right sides together, and sew along the long edge. Open and press the seam allowances.

2. Spread the backing wrong side up, and tape the edges down with masking tape. (If you are working on carpet, you can use T-pins to secure the backing to the carpet.) Center the batting on top, smoothing out any folds. Place the quilt top right side up on top of the batting and backing, making sure it is centered.

3. If you plan to machine quilt, pin baste the quilt layers together with safety pins placed about 3˝–4˝ apart. Begin basting in the center, and move toward the edges first in vertical, then horizontal, rows. Try not to pin directly on the intended quilting lines.

If you plan to hand quilt, baste the layers together with thread using a long needle and light-colored thread. Knot one end of the thread. Using stitches approximately the length of the needle, begin in the center and move out toward the edges in vertical and horizontal rows approximately 4˝ apart. Add 2 diagonal rows of basting.

4. Quilt as desired. Remember to check your batting manufacturer's recommendations for how close the quilting lines must be.

Binding with Rickrack

1. Trim the excess batting and backing even with the edges of the quilt top.

2. Draw a line ¼˝ in from the raw front edge of your quilt with a pencil. The line you just drew will be your placement line for the rickrack. Stitch the rickrack into place following your line, making sure you are stitching down the center of the rickrack. Do not miter the rickrack; trim it at each corner, and attach a new piece for the next side. (You can also choose to finish the binding without rickrack. In that case, follow Step 1 and Steps 3–9 of this section.)

3. Piece the binding strips together to make a continuous binding strip. Trim the seam allowance to ¼˝. Press the seams open.

4. Press the entire strip in half lengthwise with wrong sides together, being careful not to stretch the bias edges. With the raw edges even, pin the binding to the front edge of the quilt a few inches away from a corner, and leave the first few inches of the binding unattached. Start sewing using a ¼˝ seam allowance.

5. Stop ¼˝ away from the first corner (fig. A), and backstitch 1 stitch.

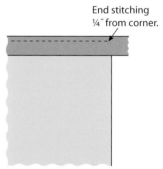

End stitching ¼˝ from corner.

A: Stitch to ¼˝ from corner.

6. Lift the presser foot and needle. Rotate the quilt one-quarter turn. Fold the binding at a right angle so it extends straight above the quilt and the fold forms a 45° angle in the corner (fig. B).

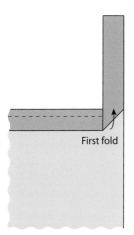

B: First fold for miter

7. Then bring the binding strip down even with the edge of the quilt (fig. C). Begin sewing at the folded edge. Repeat in the same manner at all corners.

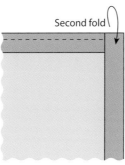

C: Second fold alignment

8. Continue stitching until you are back near the beginning of the binding strip.

9. After stitching around the quilt, fold the beginning tail of the binding strip under ¼˝, so the raw edge will be inside the binding. Place the tail end of the binding strip on top of the beginning folded end. Continue to attach the binding, and stitch slightly beyond the starting stitches. Trim off the excess binding. Fold the binding over the raw edges to the quilt back, and hand stitch, mitering the corners.

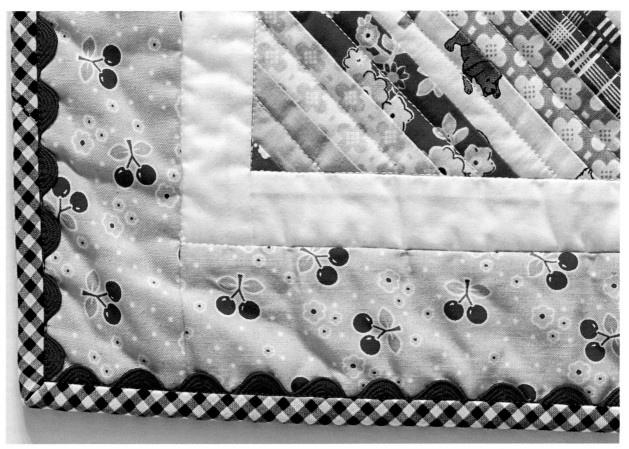

Isn't the rickrack a nice added touch?

Bonus Quilt 1: May Day

Finished quilt: 50½˝ × 62˝

Made by Jeanette White

This is an example of creating a beautiful new quilt using just one row pattern and a little imagination. It combines the ribbons from Row 2 with some simple machine appliqué for a fun throw-size spring quilt. We used a lot of fabrics in our favorite color combination—red and pink.

Materials

Ribbon row: ⅜ yard of red solid

⅞ yard of red print

½ yard of off-white solid

Borders and appliqué backgrounds: 2¼ yards of light pink solid

Leaf pairs: 12 fat quarters or quarter yards in various colors and prints

Stems: 1⅝ yards of green (You will have most of this left over for another project.)

Binding: ⅞ yard of light blue, cut into 2½˝ bias strips (You'll need about 240˝ total.)

Backing: 3¼ yards of red print

Apliquick or similar medium-weight interfacing: 1 yard

⅜˝ **bias tape maker**

Basting glue

Batting: 58˝ × 70˝

Cutting

RED SOLID

• Cut 25 squares 3¾˝ × 3¾˝.

RED PRINT

• Cut 5 strips 5˝ × WOF.

Locate the 45° angle on your ruler, and lay it on the long raw edge of your fabric near the end. Make a true cut at a 45° angle across the width of your strip (see Row 2: Ribbons, Cutting, page 18).

Lay your ruler on the raw edge of your true cut, and cut 30 diagonal strips 5˝ wide. You should get 6 pieces from each of the long strips.

OFF-WHITE SOLID

• Cut 25 squares 4⅛˝ × 4⅛˝; then cut them in half diagonally, creating 50 triangles.

LIGHT PINK SOLID

• Cut 4 strips 4½˝ × 55˝ along the LOG for the borders.

• Cut 72 rectangles 3½˝ × 5½˝ for the leaf appliqué backgrounds. You should be able to cut about 45 of them from the remainder of the 52˝ piece from the borders.

GREEN

• Cut 4 strips ⅞˝ × 55˝ along the LOG for the stems.

Ribbon Rows

Refer to Row 2: Ribbons, Stitching It All Together (page 19) to construct the ribbon rows.

1. Create a unit comprised of a red square and a pair of cream triangles. Make 25.

2. Connect these units to the red print diamonds, creating ribbon pairs. Make 25.

3. Stitch 5 pairs together to create each row. Make 5 rows.

4. You will have 5 extra red print diamonds. Stitch one to the end of each row so that there is a red print diamond at the start and finish.

5. Use the 45° angle on your ruler to align with the last diamond's diagonal seam. Trim to square-off all 5 rows at each end at a perfect right angle.

Appliqué Leaf Rows

1. Using the leaf appliqué pattern (below), trace 144 leaves onto the non-shiny side of the Apliquick or similar interfacing, and cut out on the exact traced line.

2. Press 12 interfacing leaves onto the wrong side of each of 12 fat quarters, making sure to leave at least ¾˝ for the seam allowances between them.

3. Cut out all 144 leaves from the fat quarters, with a ¼˝ seam allowance outside of the interfacing.

4. Machine appliqué (see Row 9: Flying Geese, Appliqué Flowers, page 49) to stitch down matching leaf pairs onto each of the 72 pink rectangles. You'll use each fabric 6 times.

5. Stitch 18 appliqué leaf rectangles into a row. Make 4 rows.

6. Run all 4 green stem strips through your bias tape maker, following its directions.

7. Glue-baste the stems in place, and stitch down with the machine appliqué stitch used on Row 3 (see Zigzag Appliqué Stitch, page 23).

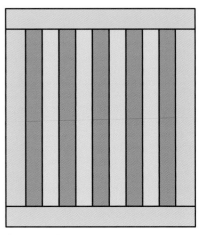

Quilt assembly

Assemble the Quilt

1. Stitch the center rows together. Start and end with a ribbon row, alternating with the appliqué stem rows. See the leaf appliqué pattern and placement diagram (at left).

2. Add 2 of the 4½˝ pink borders to the sides of the quilt, and then add the other 2 borders to the top and bottom (see Putting It All Together, Borders, page 62).

Finishing

Layer, baste, machine quilt as desired, and attach the binding (see Putting It All Together, Finishing and Binding with Rickrack, page 62). You can add or omit the rickrack. Voilà!

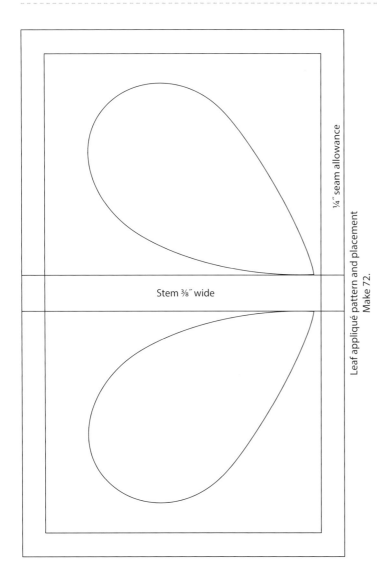

Stem ⅜˝ wide

¼˝ seam allowance

Leaf appliqué pattern and placement
Make 72.

Bonus Quilt 2: Posy Patch

Finished quilt: 62¼" × 73¼"

Made by Jeanette White and quilted by Karen Morgan

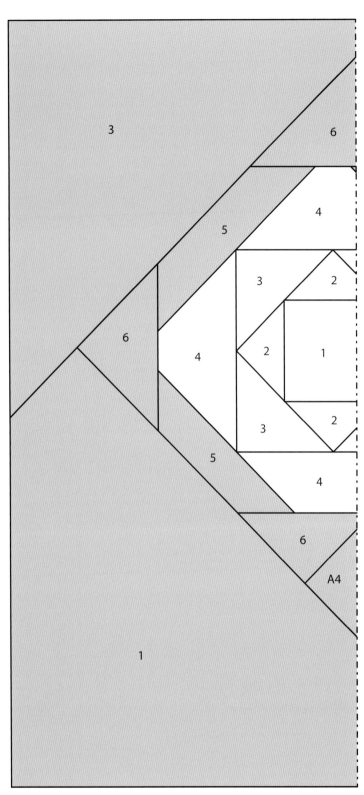

Diagonal Posy block

Materials

Paper-pieced flowers and center squares: 26 fat quarters in a variety of colors, 6 of which should be different hues of green

Flower backgrounds: 3½ yards of off-white solid

Borders: 2⅛ yards of gray print

Backing: 4¼ yards

Vellum sheets: 64 for paper piecing

Template plastic: 2 sheets

Batting: 69˝ × 80˝

Binding: ⅞ yard, cut into 2½˝ bias strips (You'll need about 285˝ total.)

Cutting

FAT QUARTERS

- Cut 5 squares 4½˝ × 4½˝ from each of the 26 fat quarters.

GRAY PRINT

- Cut 2 strips 1⅝˝ × 42˝ on the LOG for the top and bottom inner borders.

- Cut 2 strips 2⅛˝ × 56˝ on the LOG for the side inner borders.

- Cut 4 strips 2˝ × 75˝ on the LOG for the outer borders.

Center Patchwork

1. Arrange the 4½˝ × 4½˝ squares into 13 rows of 10 squares each. Either take a photo on your phone or mark the placement with masking tape to ensure an even spread of colors and hues.

2. Stitch the squares into rows. Press the seams of the even-numbered rows to the right and the odd-numbered rows to the left.

3. Stitch the rows together, making sure your seams are butting correctly as you go, to create your quilt center.

Paper-Pieced Flowers for Borders

1. Make 28 large and 32 small paper-pieced posy flowers (see Row 6: Posy Flowers, page 34). Use fat quarters for the flowers and off-white fabric for all the background pieces.

2. Make 4 Diagonal Posy corner blocks using the same paper-piecing method. (You will need to trace the pattern onto 2 sheets of paper and tape them together.)

3. Stitch together 7 large and 10 small flowers to create a side border (see the quilt photo for placement). Repeat for the second side border.

4. Stitch together 7 large and 6 small flowers to create the top border. Repeat to create the bottom border.

5. Stitch a Diagonal Posy corner block to both ends of the top and bottom borders.

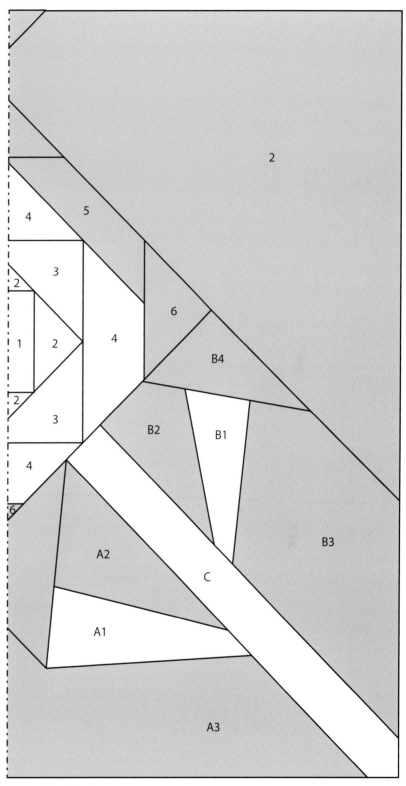

Diagonal Posy block

Borders

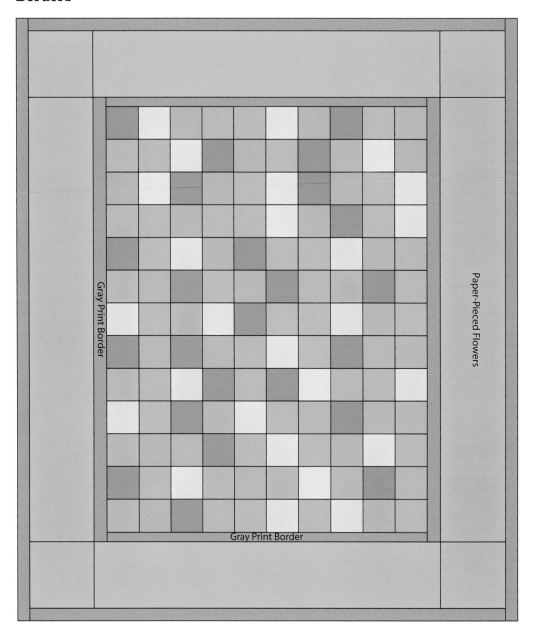

1. Stitch the inner border to the quilt: the top and bottom first and then the sides (see Putting It All Together, Borders, page 62). Press the seams toward the border.

2. Stitch the paper-pieced flower border to the quilt: the side border first and then the top and bottom borders. Press these seams toward the inner border.

3. Stitch the outer border to the quilt: the top and bottom first and then the sides. Press the seams toward the outer borders. Phew! That one was a lot of work, but so worth it!

Finishing

Layer, baste, machine quilt as desired, and attach the binding (see Putting It All Together, Finishing and Binding with Rickrack, page 62). You can add or omit the rickrack. Voilà!

About the Authors

Jeanette White and Erin Hamilton are partners in everything quilting. For fifteen years, they had a successful brick-and-mortar quilt shop called Piper's Quilts & Comforts in Salt Lake City, Utah, a featured Better Homes & Gardens Top 10 Shop. They decided to close the shop in 2015 to allow more time for the creative aspect of the industry, and they currently design patterns under the name Piper's Girls. Piper is a family name and a family business: Jeanette is Erin's mother-in-law. Visit their blog at pipersgirls.com.

Want even more creative content?

Go to ctpub.com/offer

& sign up to receive our gift to you!

Make it, snap it, share it *using #ctpublishing*